DESTINED TO SOAR

So a book of remembrance was written before Him
*For those who fear the L*ORD
And who meditate on His name.
*"They shall be Mine," says the L*ORD *of hosts,*
"On the day that I make them My jewels.
And I will spare them
As a man spares his own son who serves him."

—*Malachi 3:16–17*

DESTINED

to

SOAR

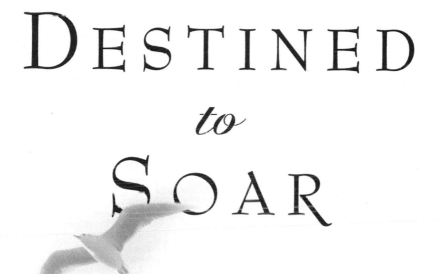

K.P.Yohannan

BOOKS

A DIVISION OF GOSPEL FOR ASIA
WWW.GFA.ORG

ISBN 978-1-59589-058-0

Library of Congress Control Number: 2009938157

Published by gfa books, a division of Gospel for Asia
1800 Golden Trail Court, Carrollton, TX 75010 USA
Phone: (972) 300–7777
Fax: (972) 300–7778

Printed in the United States of America

For more information about other materials, visit our website: www.gfa.org.

09 10 11 12 13 14 15 / 5 4 3 2 1

To Keith Vanden Heuvel,
who is a faithful servant of the Lord
and in his own quiet way
of serving Him
makes a huge difference in our generation.

Table of Contents

Acknowledgments

I am deeply grateful to Gisela for doing the primary editing work for this book and then also to Teresa, Kim, Heidi, Cindy, Tricia, Luci, Brenda and Hannah for the part each one played to make this book a reality. May the Lord reward you for your labor of love.

Introduction

God gave us a promise in His Word that those who know Him and are seeking His face will soar like eagles (see Isaiah 40:31). We were made to fly. But so often we instead feel like we are tripping over potholes on the ground rather than taking flight. It is *a journey* to the sky. There are many lessons that aid us to rise above the clouds, and you'll find some of them written on the pages of this book.

I invite you to embark on this journey. It is both stretching and enriching. There will be many signposts along the way pointing us to the One who transforms us into His own image. It won't happen within a day or a week or even months. There will be times of introspection that will result in cleansing and wholesomeness. It will mean giving up personal, hidden agendas for His sake. This is a call to become a people who really know God.

God is looking for those who will be His, not just workers. Christianity is full of workers—but He doesn't easily find individuals who have given up every right to run their own lives and be completely His.

Would you choose that road? I guarantee you, He will lift you up. I guarantee you, He will bless you. I guarantee you, you will not be destroyed. I guarantee you, it is grace and blessing and a wonderful journey ahead. This is His promise.

This journey is not about rules and regulations and directives. It is a sense of living with another world on the inside of us. It is then that we can truly soar above the weight of this world. Will you join me on this journey?

CHAPTER 1

Destined to Soar

A tiny eaglet fell out of his nest in a tall tree near a farm, and he landed in a chicken coop. He found himself surrounded by little chicks and thought they were his siblings. He grew up like them, learning to scratch for insects and peck at the seeds the farmer scattered in the barnyard.

The young eagle's wings and feathers began to grow, but he never perceived himself to be anything more than a member of his chicken family. One day an older eagle, soaring in the sky, spotted him in the barnyard. The eagle swooped down and had a face-to-face talk with the young eagle. "You are not a chicken," he said. "You are an eagle. You are not supposed to hop around on the ground looking for bugs. This is not your life. You are meant to fly in the heavens and ride the wind."

These words opened the little eagle's eyes to who he really was and gave him the desire to join his new friend above the clouds. He spread his wings and, after a few attempts to lift off, flew to the nearest tree. With each try he flew farther and higher; before long, he mounted up with the wind and disappeared into the vastness and freedom of the sky.

This story illustrates how we as believers are meant to live up to our God-given potential. It also teaches us that the foundation for our behavior and success comes from our understanding of who we are in Christ.

Jesus is our forerunner and our example. How did He build a strong foundation of who He was? When we look at Scripture, we see that it was no easy road for Him. Throughout His ministry, Jesus faced temptations from Satan, severe accusations from His enemies, attacks on His life, slander from religious leaders, blasphemy charges from the Pharisees, concerns about His sanity from His family and desertions from His followers.

He was 100 percent human, but without sin. Any one of these things could have plunged Him into deep emotional turmoil, severe doubts about His messiahship and questions about whether He had correctly interpreted the Scriptures regarding His mission on earth.

Yet the Gospels show us that Jesus never had an identity crisis. On the contrary, He knew—absolutely and without a doubt—who He was. No matter what happened to Him and around Him, His understanding of Himself never changed.

He told the Jews: "For I know where I came from and where I am going; but you do not know where I come from and where I am going. . . . For I proceeded forth and came from God; nor have I come of Myself, but He sent Me" (John 8:14, 42).

And without hesitation Jesus said of Himself: "I am the bread of life. . . . I am the light of the world. . . . I am the good shepherd. . . . I am the resurrection and the life. . . . I am the way, the truth, and the life. No one comes to the Father except through Me" (John 6:35, 8:12, 10:11, 11:25, 14:6). Both Jesus' intimate relationship with God the Father and His earthly ministry were rooted in His complete understanding of His identity. It became the unshakable foundation for the course of His life on earth.

This foundation gave Jesus immense strength to face His problems and battles. In the midst of severe temptations in the wilderness, Jesus could have accepted Satan's offers to turn stones into bread, jump from the tower and worship him to acquire all the kingdoms of the earth without going to the cross. Yet Jesus refused—because He *knew* who He was.

No matter what Jesus faced, He lived by what He knew about Himself, not by what others thought or said about Him. As the Son of God, Jesus subjected Himself to the Father in all things. That's why He was always seeking His Father's will and consulting with Him about His mission on earth instead of listening to the expert advice of those around Him. He said: "I do nothing of Myself; but as My Father taught Me, I speak these things. . . . For I always do those things that please Him" (John 8:28–29).

> ~ *No matter what* Jesus *faced, He* lived *by what He knew about Himself, not by what others thought about Him.* ~

The Jews were constantly after Jesus to figure out whether He was their awaited Messiah. They tested Him with questions, looked for signs, and compared Him and His ministry with their expectations.

Jesus found His identity in Scripture and always directed these people to the Scriptures and the prophecies that spoke of Him. He first established His identity in His hometown of Nazareth when He preached in the synagogue there. He read the passage in Isaiah that described the Messiah's ministry:

"The Spirit of the Lord is upon Me, because He has anointed Me to preach the gospel to the poor; He has sent Me to heal the brokenhearted, to proclaim liberty to the captives and recovery of sight to the blind, to set at liberty those who are oppressed; to proclaim the acceptable year of the Lord" (Luke 4:18–19).

Then He said to His audience, "Today this Scripture is fulfilled in your hearing" (Luke 4:21).

As we, too, believe and understand our position in Christ, it will revolutionize our thinking, our walk with God and our service to Him. Like Him, we must go to the Word of God and find our identity in what it says about us. And when we face our battles, the knowledge of who we are will fill us with tremendous strength and the assurance that as sons and daughters of the Living God, we indeed will be more than overcomers.

Take courage: Stand in the truth of who you are.

CHAPTER 2

Keep Looking at What Jesus Is Doing

John the Baptist sat in Herod's prison. Knowing that his life hung by a very thin thread, he sent two of his disciples to Jesus to ask, "Are You the Coming One, or do we look for another?" (Luke 7.20). What had happened to the mighty, fearless preacher who called his whole nation to repentance and accused the Pharisees of being a brood of vipers?

John was born to elderly parents—an incredible miracle. Growing up, he must have heard them say countless times, "You are the one the prophet Isaiah wrote about, the one who will come in the spirit of Elijah to prepare the way of the LORD." John had absolutely no doubt about his identity, and he knew how to answer those who asked if he was the Messiah. "I am not the Christ," he confessed. "I am the voice of one crying in the wilderness. . . . It is He who, coming after me, is preferred before me" (John 1:20, 23, 27).

Shortly afterward, John publicly declared Jesus to be the Son of God and Israel's Messiah, proclaiming, "Behold! The Lamb of God who takes away the sin of the world!"

(John 1:29). This declaration testifies of the deep knowledge, revelation, conviction and understanding John had about God's purpose.

In prison, however, he wondered whether or not he had made a fatal mistake. John the Baptist—of whom Jesus testified that he was the greatest man born on earth (see Matthew 11:11)—went through the worst confusion and doubt anyone can entertain: He questioned whether he'd failed his mission and misled his nation by declaring the wrong person to be the Messiah.

The reason for his confusion was that he expected Jesus to use His power to rescue him and set up His kingdom.

Amazingly, Jesus didn't condemn him. Neither did He say to John's disciples, "You mean John sent you to ask Me these questions? It shows that he has lost it completely. I never thought he would fall by the wayside like anyone else." Instead, Jesus responded with understanding and compassion. First, He healed many who were sick, blind and lame, and He delivered those afflicted with evil spirits.

Then He told John's disciples, "Go and tell John the things you have seen and heard: that the blind see, the lame walk, the lepers are cleansed, the deaf hear, the dead are raised, the poor have the gospel preached to them. And blessed is he who is not offended because of Me" (Luke 7:22–23).

What Jesus was saying to John was this: "John, it's all right. You are expecting Me to snap My fingers and get you out of prison and vindicate you. You are a righteous and wonderful individual, but that's not what I am going to do.

"When you serve Me, you will go through times of deep struggles. But if you keep looking at what I, the Lord, am doing, you will see that you have a part in all of it.

"John, don't forget that these blind people now see, the crippled walk and millions who were lost and bound for hell are turning to the Father. John, it's worth it."

> *"If you keep looking at what I, the Lord, am* doing, *you will see that you have a part in all of it."*

Jesus didn't chide John for his doubt, but He encouraged him and strengthened his arms. How do we deal with others when they go through struggles?

When I was younger, I remember how aggressive, proud and absolutely certain I was about everything. I used to be so critical and judgmental toward other brothers and sisters who were going through difficult times full of doubt and confusion. Some of them wanted to quit the ministry. Instead of showing compassion for them, I would come up with Bible verses to preach at them.

Sometimes I did the same thing to my wife. One day, when I came home, her eyes were all red, and I asked her what was wrong. But before she could answer, I told her five Scripture references.

"Can you please stop preaching at me?" she asked. "I know all these Bible verses myself. The whole day I struggled with the kids and things at home. All I want is for you to understand what I am going through."

Let us learn from Jesus!

The next time we see our brother or sister discouraged and confused, let us not say with our mouth, "I will pray for you," while in our heart we are saying, "You creep, don't you know better?" Instead, let us encourage them to keep looking at what Jesus is doing and see the difference that their lives are making for the kingdom of God.

And one more thing: When Jesus talked to the crowds about John, He never mentioned John's doubt and confusion. Instead, He made the most amazing statements about John's life and ministry.

Can we do the same with our brothers and sisters? Let us be willing to forget their problems and times of discouragement and see only the amazing things God has done in and through their lives. And then let us believe that He will do even greater things through them in the future.

Will you be God's instrument of compassion and encouragement?

Chapter 3

Follow Him in Humility

A well-known preacher flies into town for a citywide crusade. He expects to be greeted at the airport by a delegation of prestigious individuals. Instead, an old taxi driver holding a piece of cardboard with the preacher's name misspelled waits at baggage claim and then drops him off at a second-class hotel. The room is small, the bed uncomfortable, the service lousy, and there is not even a fruit basket or welcome note. When no one calls or takes him out to dinner, he feels deeply offended and says to himself, "How dare they treat me like this? Don't they know who I am? They don't deserve my ministry. That's the last time I'm coming to this place."

The next morning, however, all his honor and good fortunes are quickly restored after the organizers discover that their guest speaker had become a victim of miscommunication.

Could it be that this incident was not an unfortunate mix-up, but rather the Lord testing His servant's humility? After all, He had sent this man to represent Himself, the Christ of the New Testament. And in the Gospels, we see so clearly that Jesus was genuinely humble in His dealings with others.

What was the key to Christ's humility? It was deeply rooted in His understanding and accepting the truth that the greatest glory in heaven and on earth is to be the servant of all. That's the reason why prophetic passages like Isaiah 53 portray Him as a servant, and Psalm 40:8 describes Him saying: "I delight to do Your will, O my God."

◯ *The* greatest glory *in heaven and on earth is to be the* servant *of all.* ◯

If there is no greater glory than being a servant of all, then much of our 21st-century Church is miles away from the pattern Christ left us. Our worldly view of glory is precisely where we need to get our understanding set straight.

The moment we realize that it is God's will for us to follow Christ's humility, we often get this negative feeling that we are about to become a broken, selfless creature everyone can trample on.

However, the humility God calls us to is far more than being broken from our pride and sin. It is something entirely positive and wonderful. It is participating in the very nature of Jesus.

Pride caused Lucifer, the most beautiful, powerful and intelligent angel, to fall and become Satan, who led man into sin. And it was Christ's humility that saved and lifted fallen man from the pit of hell to sit on His throne with Him. Shouldn't that amazing truth give us enough reason to follow Christ's humility?

When we seek to follow Christ and become like Him, we often start by making a long list of spiritual exercises we plan to do to make it happen. However, the foundation of becoming like Christ in humility—as well as in all other virtues—begins with this one step: "Take My yoke upon you" (Matthew 11:29).

If I carry a yoke on my neck, it means that I no longer stand up straight. I once saw a postcard with the words "Not I, but Christ" written on it. To illustrate, the artist had drawn a man standing up tall inside the letter "I." Then he drew the same man inside the letter "C," but now the man had to bend over to fit.

This humility of Christ will not become a reality in my life by accident, by wishing for it, by studying about it or by fasting and praying for it. It only comes by my deliberate willingness to obey what Jesus told me to do: to take His yoke upon me. That means from now on, Jesus and I are yoked together. Where He goes, I go; where He turns, I turn; when He stops to comfort a widow, bless a child or wash His disciples' feet, I do the same.

As I learn from Him how to walk under His yoke, I discover that the yoke is easy and my heart is at peace. And by submitting to His yoke and imitating Him, His gentleness and humility will become mine.

My dear friend, will you take this first step today and decide to take His yoke upon you? There is no other way to develop the humility that represents the Lord Jesus.

Follow Him in humility.

CHAPTER 4

"I Thought . . ."

Naaman was raging with anger. He had traveled all the way from Syria with chariots full of gold, silver and expensive gifts for Elisha—and now the prophet wouldn't even grant him a one-minute audience. And what was worse, Elisha's servant passed a message to him that he should dip seven times in the Jordan River to be healed of his leprosy (see 2 Kings 5:9–12).

It was a simple, inexpensive ritual he was supposed to perform. No one could make fun of him because he was far away from his homeland.

But the mighty captain of the Syrian army was not about to follow these stupid instructions. Why? These instructions were not his own thoughts.

In his fury, Naaman exclaimed, "Behold, *I thought,* He will surely come out to me, and stand, and call on the name of the LORD his God, and strike his hand over the place, and recover the leper" (2 Kings 5:11, KJV, emphasis mine).

However, the servants of Naaman realized that their master was about to pass up his only possible chance to get healed. Fearing they had made the long trip with all its hardship and headache for nothing, they pleaded with him. Naaman finally calmed down, obeyed the prophet's instructions and experienced the healing power of the God of Israel (see 2 Kings 5:13).

Here's the frightening truth: Naaman came as a leper and was about to go back as a leper, to live a lonely, rejected, depressed and forsaken life. In the end he would have died of his disease, *all because he thought the wrong thoughts.*

This can be our experience as well!

Our own thoughts are one of the greatest enemies of a life of faith that honors God.

We may pray, fast, agonize, weep and cry out to God about a matter, but we receive no answer. Why? Like Naaman, we cling to our own thoughts as to how God should go about answering our request. And with our boundaries, we tie the hands of God and prevent Him from moving on our behalf.

> ～ *Our own* **thoughts**
> *are one of the greatest* **enemies**
> *of a life of faith that honors God.* ～

Isaiah 55:6–11 gives us a clear picture of how much the Living God wants to abundantly pardon, bless us, answer our prayers and fulfill His wonderful promises. But those who come to Him must give up one thing: their own thoughts. "Let the wicked forsake his way, and the unrighteous man his thoughts; let him return to the LORD, and He will have mercy on him" (Isaiah 55:7).

In the following verses, God gives us the reason why it is so important for us to give up our own thoughts: " 'For

My thoughts are not your thoughts, nor are your ways My ways,' says the LORD. 'For as the heavens are higher than the earth, so are My ways higher than your ways, and My thoughts than your thoughts' " (Isaiah 55:8–9).

Then God goes on explaining that His Word (or His thoughts) works just as the rain and the snow that come down from heaven and bring forth fruit: "So shall My word be that goes forth from My mouth; it shall not return to Me void, but it shall accomplish what I please, and it shall prosper in the thing for which I sent it" (Isaiah 55:11).

The whole message God wants to tell us is that if we want to experience God, we must first abandon our thoughts and then start thinking His.

Why aren't our thoughts as believers in Jesus automatically in alignment with God's thoughts? The Apostle Paul explains that our natural mind is always in opposition to God and what He thinks: "Because the carnal mind is enmity against God; for it is not subject to the law of God, nor indeed can be" (Romans 8:7).

You see, when we were born again, our spirit was regenerated by the Holy Spirit, but the house is still the same. That means our body and our mind, left to themselves, will continue in their old ways. That's why the Bible tells us clearly what we must do to bring both of them into subjection to God: " . . . that you present your bodies a living sacrifice, holy, acceptable to God. . . . And do not be conformed to this world, but be transformed by the renewing of your mind" (Romans 12:1–2).

It is our responsibility, not God's, to get our mind renewed. How? We renew our minds by changing our entire thought process through God's Word.

Naaman the Syrian first had to align his thinking with the word of God spoken to him by the prophet Elisha *before* he could receive God's answer to his problem.

We too must make the same decision. If we want to see victory over the sin with which we struggle, our families saved, our needs met and this world won to Christ in our lifetime, we must consciously choose to abandon all our own natural (and even religious) thoughts and begin to think God's thoughts. All things are possible with God if we believe—as God thinks.

Believe Him!

CHAPTER 5

The Potter Works Only
with *Soft Clay!*

When I was a boy, growing up in India, I often went to a potter's house near my high school. I was fascinated watching him make clay vessels. During those visits, I never saw the potter take a hardened lump of clay and put it on his wheel to make something out of it. He, like every other potter in the world, used only soft and tender clay to work with. So does God!

The prophet Jeremiah tells us that God is like a potter and His people are the clay that He wants to form into a beautiful vessel. In order to accomplish this, God looks for soft and pliable hearts.

Man measures the quality and usefulness of a person by his education, ability and expertise. Yet God determines a person's true value by the condition of his or her heart: "Man looks at the outward appearance, but the LORD looks at the heart" (1 Samuel 16:7, NIV).

I used to watch that same potter soften the clay. Day after day he would pour water on it and pound it thoroughly until it became soft. It took God 20 long years of "pouring and pounding" until Jacob's heart became soft enough. Moses needed 40 years of desert life to become the meekest man on earth (see Numbers 12:3, KJV), who could then lead Israel out of Egypt.

Hebrews 3:15 says, "Today, if you will hear His voice, do not harden your hearts." This verse tells us that when God works in our lives and speaks to us, we have a choice. Will we choose to soften our hearts to His work in us, or will we harden our hearts to Him and the circumstances He is allowing?

In fact, it is possible for us as believers to have a tender heart for a season, but then slowly turn and allow our hearts to become hard. This is a scary place to be. We can go years before we really begin to recognize the symptoms.

But the Lord will not just let us go. He will allow circumstances to pound us so our hearts will once again become soft and pliable. The people of Israel are the perfect example of this. Just think of how many times God allowed them to face famines, hardships, oppression, defeat and captivity in order to soften their hearts and help them return to Him!

The Lord will not just let us go.
He will **allow** **circumstances** *to pound us*
so our hearts will once again
become **soft** *and pliable.*

How should we respond to God in this process? We should yield to His work and not make it more difficult for Him. The Enemy works constantly to lure us to the place in which we harden our hearts. It must be our highest priority to keep our hearts with all diligence (see Proverbs 4:23). No matter how long we've traveled or how soft our hearts are right now, we have the choice just around the corner to allow either blessings or trials to harden our hearts. That's why Proverbs says "with all diligence." Keeping our hearts will not happen casually.

What are some of the potholes we may run into along the way?

Out of all the temptations, I believe the worst is having *an elevated view of ourselves*. Whether it is something significant we did for the kingdom or an area in which we feel superior, we can easily slip into feeling important and not recognize that our hearts are filled with pride, arrogance and an exalted view of ourselves.

We must remind ourselves that all the gifts, talents and ministry we have are given to us by the Lord. It's all God's grace. Look for opportunities to humble yourself. Choose to submit to one another (see Ephesians 5:21) and lay down your own preferences for the sake of others. Don't fight for your rights, and be willing to give up something. Grace is given to those who are humble (see James 4:6), not to those who are right or feel indispensable.

A hardened heart is contagious. Unless we are careful to guard our hearts, we will be poisoned by others' *negative attitudes and talk*. It can begin with one person in a church or ministry who is dissatisfied, bitter, critical and unwilling to change. Soon the atmosphere of love among the brothers and sisters is replaced by disunity, anger and hardness of heart toward each other and the Lord.

Don't keep company with these people who sow disunity. Love them and pray for them, but have no part with them. You and I are not strong enough to withstand the poison they spread. It's in the atmosphere, and we breathe it in whether we intend to or not.

Be especially careful to whom you go to receive your counsel. Don't go to a brother or sister who is not mature in the Lord and who will sympathize and agree with your complaints and tears. Go instead to someone who is mature enough to help you see the hand of God and His purpose behind the things you face.

Any form of rebellion is like a tiny seed that, if not dealt with, will grow and eventually harden our heart and bring destruction. You must stamp it out as soon as you see it, whether it starts in your own mind or someone else's words. Don't let it linger. It will ultimately bring forth death in your life.

Maintaining the tenderness of your heart and humility depends on your *honesty before God.* Repent and run to the cross—a thousand times a day if need be. Whenever you seek the limelight, want to take credit, get hurt or have your expectations unfulfilled and your plans not work out, don't fight; go to the cross.

God always seeks to do one thing with us on the Potter's wheel—not to make us more powerful and famous, but to make us more like His Son, the Lord Jesus.

Are you that pliable clay?

CHAPTER 6

Making Decisions

Abraham had just heard God's voice telling him to leave his country, his relatives and his father's house and go to a land God would show him.

How was Abraham going to make the right decision? Logic told him to stay where he was and not listen to mysterious voices. Furthermore, for him to leave his relatives and father's house would mean that he had no one to protect and rescue him should he get in serious trouble. Besides, it made no sense to trade his present affluence and comfortable lifestyle for a harsh, nomadic existence.

It's amazing that in spite of all these reasons, Abraham still decided to walk away from everything he knew and follow God's call to the Promised Land. What caused him to make the right decision?

It was the fact that he did not look to the present with all its comforts and benefits—but rather to the future and to the far greater blessings God promised him: "I will make you a great nation; I will bless you and make your name great. . . . In you all the families of the earth shall be blessed. . . . All the land which you see I give to you and your descendants forever" (Genesis 12:2–3, 13:15).

We, too, make decisions every day: what college we should attend, whom we should marry, where we should live, how we should spend our money, what we should do with our time, in what way we should serve the Lord—and a thousand other choices.

We can learn a vital lesson about making the right decisions from Abraham: The most significant element in making the right decision is considering not the present condition, but the future. In other words, what does our decision mean for the kingdom of God and in the light of eternity?

> ~ *The most significant element in making the* right decision *is considering not the present condition, but the* future. ~

Although Abraham received God's glorious promises for the future, some of these promises were still decades—and others, centuries—away from becoming reality. What did Abraham do in the meantime? He lived in anticipation of seeing these promises fulfilled, and he made his daily decisions by faith, in preparation for what he believed was going to happen in the future.

> By faith Abraham obeyed when he was called to go out to the place which he would receive as an inheritance. And he went out, not knowing where he was going. By faith he dwelt in the land of promise as in a foreign country, dwelling in tents with Isaac and Jacob, the heirs with him of the same promise; for he waited

for the city which has foundations, whose builder and maker is God (Hebrews 11:8–10).

Abraham acted just like one of the rice farmers in my village in India, who right after the monsoon season prepares his paddy field with his water buffaloes. Then he sows the seeds all over the field. He cannot see them, though, because the field is flooded. But if he just waits a few weeks, all the little green plants will come up; and if he waits a few more months, he will reap a rice harvest.

In ministry as well as in our personal life, even though we've planted the right crop, it doesn't guarantee there won't be trials along the way. Often when we encounter difficulties, inconvenience, pain and relationship problems, our immediate reaction is to second-guess the decisions we made. And if things don't change in our favor soon, we walk away, telling ourselves that it must not have been God's will after all.

Abraham was different. Although he encountered hardship, famine, enemies, war, personal failures, family problems, 25 years of waiting for a son and the Mount Moriah test in his Promised Land, he never reversed his decision and quit his life of faith.

And what happened? God used each of these difficulties to teach him, change him and cause his faith to grow stronger.

If we determine to stick with the right decision regardless of the adversities we face, God will use each one of our trials for a greater purpose. Our character will become more Christlike, our faith will grow, and we will become more useful for God's kingdom.

My dear brothers and sisters, only eternity will prove

and show what our life meant here on earth. When Abraham made his decision, I don't think he had a comprehensive understanding of the significance of his choice. In fact, I think he was surprised when he went to heaven and learned the significance of his role in God's purpose for the nation of Israel, for the coming of the Savior of the world and for us, the Bride of Christ.

In 100 years from now, what are the things that will really matter in our own lives? May this understanding strengthen our resolve to give our life—our all—to see Christ's greatest dream and ambition fulfilled: "to seek and to save that which was lost" (Luke 19:10).

Are you living for your eternal future?

CHAPTER 7

What Keeps Us Going?

I am always intrigued when I watch the start of the marathon during the summer Olympics. All the runners appear to be in top physical shape, excited to represent their countries and determined to win the gold medal.

However, it's an entirely different story when I watch them 15 or 20 miles later. They look exhausted from the hot sun that beats down on them or miserable because of rain that makes their road slippery. Some have trouble breathing when the race takes them over a mountain, and others struggle to keep up with the fast pace.

Although everyone, no matter how long it takes them to cross the finish line, is celebrated with cheers and applause, some runners will never get there. Somewhere along the route they drop out of the race due to exhaustion, injury or discouragement.

In the marathon race and in our Christian life, persevering until the end is what it's all about, not just starting well. What do I mean? Don't give up your walk with Jesus; endure in the call He gave you to win this lost world and build His kingdom.

Like the marathon runners, we, too, will encounter

adversities along the way that could cause us to quit the race. What are some of these adversities?

- Relationship problems with other Christians that severely threaten our treasured self-life.

- Physical and financial setbacks that cause us to lose hope.

- Lack of apparent fruit and thus fulfillment in our service to the Lord.

- Facing our latent failures and sins that expose our unbrokenness, pride, selfishness, stubbornness or critical spirit.

- Frustration when serving the Lord becomes hard work and the feelings are gone.

- Feeling inadequate and overwhelmed by the expectations of others.

- Spiritual dryness that comes when God tests us to see if we will still walk with Him by faith, even when there is nothing within or without to support us.

- Losing sight of our priorities—shifting from serving the Lord to protecting our self-interests.

I have served the Lord full-time for the past 40 years. From my own life and experience, I can tell you this: The godliest Christian leaders I have met, the most challenging sermons I have heard and the best books I have read on evangelism and discipleship have not been enough to help me survive in the race!

Only one thing has kept me in the ministry and following Christ, and that is learning and practicing what the writer of Hebrews said: "Let us run with endurance the race that is set before us, looking unto Jesus, the author and finisher of our faith" (Hebrews 12:1–2).

The secret of our survival is fixing our eyes on Jesus and making Him alone our focus. Then our walk with God and our commitment to serve Him will no longer depend on whether or not people treat us right or circumstances are in our favor. We will no longer rely on our emotions to support us or on our successes to keep us going. Jesus alone will become our goal and motivation—our prize—and we will live for Him, run our race for Him and cross the finish line for Him.

> *Unless you learn to fix your eyes*
> *on **Jesus alone**, you will have no stability*
> *in your walk with God.*

My dear friend, unless you learn to fix your eyes on Jesus alone, you will have no stability in your walk with God or in your service to Him.

Jesus Himself said, "Follow Me."

Therefore, meditate on Him, consider Him and think about Him so that you may not grow weary in your heart. The answer to enduring until the end is not self-effort or a rational attempt to figure out the answers, but rather to stop and look into His eyes.

If we do this, all the things that surround us in this world will become shadows in the light of Him. After all his struggles, Job found the answer he was searching for when he fell on his face and worshiped the Lord.

Look to Him. He's waiting for you.

CHAPTER 8

Striving for Unity

The whole world agrees we are in need of peace and unity. Governments turn to force and strict laws to keep people from destroying each other. On a much smaller scale, millions of families and married couples have their own difficulties as they seek to find enough common ground to live in peace with each other.

God, on the other hand, expects Christians to "be like-minded, having the same love, being of one accord, of one mind" (Philippians 2:2, KJV).

Why is unity so important to God? Paul Billheimer explains the reason in his book *Destined for the Throne:* Before the world began, the Father wanted to find a Bride for His Son, so He created us. God didn't look for many brides, but only for *one* Bride.[1] The purpose of the cross is to make millions of people from a million different backgrounds and races into one individual—the Bride of Christ.

In the light of this high calling, it is so serious and of utmost importance that each of us is "endeavoring to keep the unity of the Spirit . . ." (Ephesians 4:3). "Endeavor" is another word for try, attempt, labor, strive, exert and struggle. Just by looking at these synonyms, it is obvious that it is a very deliberate, conscious act. We cannot simply say to one another, "Well, if you agree with what I say and if you eat the same food I like, I will sit at your table and we will have unity."

In fact, the Apostle Paul tells us in the same text of Scripture exactly what we must do to be able to attain this unity: "I . . . beseech you to walk worthy of the calling with which you were called, with all lowliness and gentleness, with longsuffering, bearing with one another in love, endeavoring to keep the unity of the Spirit in the bond of peace" (Ephesians 4:1–3). What Paul is expressing is that we should do everything we can, even at the expense of our own feelings, to maintain this unity of the Spirit.

> *We should do* everything *we can,*
> *even at the expense of our own feelings,*
> *to maintain this* unity *of the Spirit.*

We find a beautiful picture of what it takes to maintain this kind of unity in Jesus' last Passover with His disciples. When He took the bread, He said to them: " . . . this is My body which is broken for you" (1 Corinthians 11:24).

If we look closely at a piece of bread, we will find that it is made up of thousands of kernels of grain; however, none of these individual kernels was left whole. They were all ground up into powder and mixed together before a loaf of bread could be formed and baked.

The bread Jesus gave to His disciples was not only a picture of His body being broken on our behalf on the cross of Calvary, but it was equally a picture of what it took for

Jesus to become the Bread of Life. He was crushed and powdered as He laid down His own will and learned obedience
through the things He suffered.

What about us? The Bride of Christ is also the Body of
Christ. If we are His Body, we must also become bread that
God can break to feed the multitudes of our generation.

We can only become a loaf of bread to feed the hungry
if the oneness of the Spirit is among us. And oneness only
comes by yielding ourselves to be ground, powdered and
mixed together.

Will you yield yourself to Him in your own circumstances?

CHAPTER 9

Here Comes God
with the Pruning Shears

You are so excited. For the first time in your Christian walk, you have discovered a fruit of the Spirit in an area of your life in which you'd struggled for years. Just when you'd almost given up, you read John 15:5: "He who abides in Me, and I in him, bears much fruit." Suddenly you understood that the whole concept of fruit-bearing was so simple: By staying in Jesus, letting His life flow through you, the fruit would naturally grow.

Now it has actually happened. You are rejoicing, and you can't wait to show the new fruit to your Heavenly Father. To your great joy, He lets you know that He will soon come to inspect the branch in your life that has produced fruit. You can hardly wait for His arrival and suspect that He will surprise you with a certificate or a reward for doing so well.

But to your bewilderment, when He arrives He carries nothing but a pair of big pruning shears in His hands.

What is He planning to do? Somehow you get the feeling that His idea of inspecting your fruit-bearing branch doesn't exactly match your own expectations.

John 15:2 tells us what God has in mind: "Every branch that bears fruit He prunes, that it may bear more fruit." This means that He will not leave us alone but instead is determined to make us even more fruitful. His strategy is to begin a very deliberate pruning process by allowing us to encounter troubles, tribulations and difficulties. These adversities serve as His shears and pruning knife.

That doesn't sound like anything we would choose for ourselves. Often, our biggest concern is how much God is planning to cut off of our branch!

But let me tell you about the tea plantations in my native country of India. Thousands of acres are covered with beautiful, lush, deep green plants. But if you were to visit these same tea estates during a certain time of the year, you would immediately think that something had gone very wrong. Instead of thriving bushes with healthy, growing leaves, you would only find naked little stumps with a few bare branches clinging to them. They look dead and hopeless. All of their beauty is gone. If you were to search for answers, you would find laborers with sharp knives and shears going from tree to tree and mercilessly cutting nearly everything off, while others continually haul away truckloads of green, leafy branches.

That is pruning.

When God puts His knife to our branches and begins to slice off the parts that must go, we often experience great loneliness, low emotional feelings and pain. Pruning actually creates a temporary dry spell in our spiritual life very similar to those barren tree stumps on the tea plantations. Saint John of the Cross from the 16th century termed this season of our lives "the dark night of the soul."[1]

Very often we feel confused, and we fail to understand what is going on. We pray, but God doesn't seem to hear. We fast, but our situation stays the same. We repent of every imaginable sin we could have committed, but find no answer. Discouraged and frightened, we conclude that something is wrong with our spiritual life.

This is the most dangerous time during the pruning process, and it's the one most often used by the Enemy to trip us up. He intends to deceive us into thinking that we have backslidden, have lost God's grace and should quit serving God. Or he tries to convince us to create a counterfeit spiritual life to compensate for what we think we have lost. If we believe him, we will generate all kinds of carnal activities so no one would easily discover that God's presence has left us.

But all the while, nothing is wrong with our spiritual life, and we haven't lost anything. We are just going through the pruning process.

‌*Accept the* wilderness *as necessary preparation for the future.*

If we could only recognize that it is the hand of God that holds the knife, then we would be able to do the right thing: trust in His wisdom, humble ourselves and honor Him by walking in faith rather than sight. Then we would be able to accept the wilderness, the cutting, the discipline, the loneliness and the pain as necessary preparation for the future.

As the Master Gardener, God can already see how this pruning process will bring about character changes within us, transform our nature and deepen our relationship with Him. He knows how best to care for us.

Choose to walk by faith during your "dark night of the soul."

CHAPTER 10

What Do I Get Out of It?

There is no doubt in my mind that Simon Peter and his brother Andrew became the talk of all the fishermen around the lake of Galilee when they suddenly left their nets to respond to Jesus' call: "Follow Me, and I will make you become fishers of men" (Mark 1:17).

We are greatly challenged by the willingness of these men to forsake all at a moment's notice to join a new teacher whose ministry and future were unknown.

But in one aspect, Peter and the other disciples were not so different from the rest of humanity. Later on, they inquired, "See, we have left all and followed You. Therefore what shall we have?" (Matthew 19:27).

No matter what we do in life, it's second nature to ask the question: *What do I get out of it?*

When we apply for a job, we want to know the benefits. If we send our children to an expensive school, we expect a certain quality of education in return.

Even in spiritual things we often have this mindset. A large number of people come to Christ because they want to go to heaven instead of hell or because they want their messed-up lives restored. And God is more than gracious to save and help them when they call upon His name.

Many believers who invest their lives, time or resources for a godly cause want to make sure that what they give will bring them something in return—whether it's joy, satisfaction, earthly blessings, recognition, honor from men, position or at least the guarantee of rewards in heaven.

If we are honest with ourselves, so often self-centeredness is at the bottom of what we do.

Sadly, this self-centeredness has prevented multitudes from hearing the Gospel. Even though many countries are closed or severely restricted to outside missionaries, millions of people could still be reached and thousands of churches planted by sending and supporting national missionaries. However, for much of Christianity, the deciding factor in their involvement is still, "What can we get out of it?"

At the root of their decision is this mindset: "Will the name of our denomination be on these churches? Can we initiate, execute and control the work by sending our own people? If not, we are not willing to get involved or share our resources. If the doors are closed to the traditional approach, we will be satisfied with sneaking in a few people to represent our group under the disguise of social work or tourism. Even if they get kicked out after a few months after having spent $20,000 to train and get them there, we will not change our policy."

We must recognize that we will lose this generation of unreached people if we don't have a significant commitment to share the love of Christ regardless of what we get out of it. I am not saying there is no place for short-term missions. Especially for young people, such an exposure to the lost world will have a far-reaching and powerful effect on their own lives and on their home churches as well. But what we need is a crucial priority shift.

> *We will* **lose** *this generation of* **unreached** *people if we don't have a significant* **commitment** *to share the love of Christ regardless of what we get out of it.*

You see, our desire for self-preservation—for securing our future and for making sure we personally get something out of what we do—whether secret or openly expressed, prevents us from thinking long or deeply enough to find godly answers. Instead, we cling to the traditional missions approach, no matter how ineffective it might be. And in our personal lives we seek to exchange the uncertain "follow Me" by leaving His calling or replacing our service to the Lord with something that guarantees security. Elisha's servant Gehazi and Demas, the co-worker of the Apostle Paul, are both examples of this.

Suddenly, it's our personal struggles and the question "What do I get out of it?" that take priority over millions of lost souls, eternity and our calling. Immaturity is our problem—little squabbles, difficulties, discouragement and unfulfilled expectations. These are the major reasons why people get out of the battle.

It takes godliness, spiritual maturity and faith to look past such things to the good ending that is still yet to be realized. Jesus saw beyond all His impending suffering on the cross to the joy of bringing multitudes into the kingdom, and He was willing to pay the price (see Hebrews 12:2).

One family had such vision and gave money for a van for one of our Bible colleges in India. They didn't ask what was in it for them. And God used this vehicle to become instrumental in seeing the church in that area grow from 85 to 227 people.

Four of our national missionaries were severely persecuted and almost killed in an Indian village. Yet all of them requested to return to the same place. If you would ask these young brothers what they would get out of it by going back, they would answer, "We can see by faith a church and people worshiping the Living God."

When we follow Jesus and serve Him, looking ahead by faith, we don't have to be anxious about what we will get out of it. He has already promised to meet our needs, and He remembers our labors on behalf of His kingdom: "For God is not unjust to forget your work and labor of love which you have shown toward His name" (Hebrews 6:10). He even tells us that whatever we have done to the least of His brothers, we have done to Him.

Keep your hand to the plow and don't look back. It is well worth it.

CHAPTER 11

Arm Yourself!

When the Lord calls us to serve Him, our hearts are overjoyed. We are excited and eager to do our best. But very soon we discover that things would go a whole lot smoother if circumstances would be more favorable—if finances weren't so tight, if John Doe with his strange ideas wouldn't be in leadership, if we wouldn't have to work beside Mary Major with her overbearing personality.

As time goes by, our initial excitement wears off, and the irritations, disappointments and conflicts with others seem to grow stronger. We can get to the point at which we can't take it anymore, and we either start fighting for our rights or we quietly walk off with hurt and bitterness in our hearts.

If we began with such willing and sincere hearts, how do we get to the place at which we are ready to walk away from this great privilege?

Could it be that we forgot we were in a battle that is not against flesh and blood? Instead, we end up fighting John and Mary instead of our real enemy. Did we arm ourselves correctly for the spiritual battle we entered, as Paul describes in Ephesians? If our answer is yes, what are we still missing?

I believe our answer is found in the letter the Apostle Peter wrote near the end of his life: "Therefore, since Christ suffered for us in the flesh, arm yourselves also with the same mind" (1 Peter 4:1).

Have we armed ourselves with the willingness to suffer—to the same extent that Christ suffered for us when He was on earth?

I am well aware that the idea of embracing suffering does not fit our 21st-century concept of following and serving Christ. Yet the Bible teaches that suffering for Him is our privilege: "For to you it has been granted on behalf of Christ, not only to believe in Him, but also to suffer for His sake" (Philippians 1:29).

Does that mean we all should seek out beatings and martyrdom? No, that's not what it means. The Lord wants us to arm ourselves with a mind to suffer just as He did, so the Enemy has nothing to work with to get us out of the battle.

Jesus' life is our model in this area: "Christ also suffered for us, leaving us an example, that you should follow His steps" (1 Peter 2:21). Christ did not suffer just during His three years of public ministry or the last few days of His life when He was crucified. He suffered throughout His life on earth. He who was without sin lived daily with the corruption and sinfulness of lost humanity.

His own family members said He had gone mentally insane. The religious community misunderstood Him and called Him a demon-possessed man. His disciples didn't understand Him. From birth to the cross, His life was full of pain, loneliness and constant misunderstanding. He is called a man of sorrows and acquainted with grief.

In the midst of it all, He chose to suffer in the flesh by saying no to Himself. He never fought for Himself or attacked anyone to defend His rights. And in the end, Jesus was able to say, "Not My will, but Thine," embracing the cross to fulfill His Father's will.

But what was the reason for Christ's suffering and death? It was to redeem mankind. And so it is with us. We can only become agents of redemption if we are willing to embrace suffering in the flesh—choosing to deny self and accepting death to our own desires.

We can only become agents of redemption *if we are willing to embrace* suffering *in the flesh.*

My dear friend, if you want to finish strong in your service to the Lord, then you must make a deliberate decision to arm yourself with a mind to suffer as Jesus did. It is never easy for our flesh when we choose to spend time alone in prayer, fast for several days, give up certain material possessions or perhaps follow the Lord's leading to a difficult mission field. But it's a choice we make for others.

Throughout his days as a disciple, Peter battled for his rights and the number-one position on the team. But in his letter, he tells us, in essence: "Brothers and sisters, take Jesus as your example. The moment you remove yourselves from this reality, the devil will take advantage of you. And all of a sudden, relationships break down, and revenge, bitterness and unforgiveness will take hold of you. Don't fight, don't argue, don't look for the first place for yourself. Don't look for anything. Always follow Him who suffered for you. This is the secret of staying in the battle" (see 1 Peter).

And when we do this, nothing—no circumstances, disappointments, financial problems, misunderstandings or shortcomings of leaders and co-workers—will be able to take us out of the battle!

For the sake of Jesus and His kingdom, are you prepared to suffer?

CHAPTER 12

Peace through Humility

Have you ever wondered how much of your humility and servant attitude is truly Christlike? You can easily find out—the next time you are given the opportunity to submit yourself to someone who, in your estimation, should be serving under you. How do you react? What are your thoughts and feelings? Is your heart at peace and your joy undisturbed, or do you struggle with resentment?

In one of our offices, a capable brother who had been with us for many years was asked by his superior to take on another position that carried a greater responsibility and a heavier workload. The brother felt honored by the offer and he understood how the change would benefit the overall work, but he responded, "I have great difficulties in making this change." When asked why, he replied, "I am older, and I have been here longer, and now I would have to report to someone who is younger than me. It is below my dignity. I don't think I can handle it."

The leader prayed for this brother and gave him a copy of *The Calvary Road* by Roy Hession.[1] A few days later after reading the book, which deals with brokenness and humility in a believer's life, the older brother was willing to accept his new position. And ever since, he has faithfully worked together with and reported to the younger brother.

Andrew Murray includes in his small book titled *Humility* the essence of the following text (paraphrased):

> Humility is far more than being broken because of our sin. It is participation in the very life of Jesus. Humility is the only root from which the genuine fruit of the Spirit can grow. Pride degraded the highest angels into devils. Humility on the other hand, has raised fallen men to the throne of angels. The great purpose of God in raising up a new creation is to demonstrate this great truth throughout eternity that all evil begins from pride and that all goodness springs from humility.[2]

In Ezekiel 28:11–17 and Isaiah 14:12–15, the Bible gives us an account of the creation of the archangel Lucifer and what happened to him when he abandoned humility.

The Word of God points out that Lucifer was perfect in two things: wisdom and beauty. That's about the ultimate dream someone could wish for himself. Not even Solomon, whom God granted to be the richest and wisest man under the sun, could claim to be perfect in wisdom and beauty.

The Apostle Paul had such incredible revelations and an understanding of the Word of God, yet he still says in Philippians 3:10 that his greatest desire is "that I may know Him." And when Paul lists all his accomplishments and outstanding achievements, he never mentions a word about his physical appearance. Tradition says Paul was a hopeless-looking creature: short, bald, bowlegged, hunched over and partially blind.

Yet here was Lucifer, head of the archangelic order, absolutely perfect in wisdom and beauty. But the day came when this wasn't enough for him. What happened? His heart was lifted up by pride.

Nowhere do we read that he conducted a huge rally in heaven to voice his opinion before the rest of the angels. No, he simply said in his heart—no words spoken—"I will ascend into heaven, I will exalt my throne above the stars of God. . . . I will be like the Most High" (Isaiah 14:13, 14).

And God immediately cast him down.

Through Lucifer's pride, Adam and the entire human race fell. Pride is the root of all sin and evil that came into the universe. But our salvation, redemption and recovery can only come through the humility of the second Adam—Christ.

Philippians 2:5–8 shows us the heart of Jesus, which is diametrically opposite to Lucifer's. Instead of looking for ways to go up, Jesus looked for ways to step down. He laid aside all His glory and emptied Himself to become a man. But He didn't stop there. His humility took Him much farther: "He humbled Himself and became obedient to the point of death, even the death of the cross" (Philippians 2:8).

Instead of looking for ways to go up, Jesus looked for ways to step down.

The Bible says in the following verses that this was exactly the reason why God highly exalted Him.

Seeing our struggle with pride, Jesus invites us in Matthew 11:29 to follow His example: "Take My yoke upon you and learn from Me, for I am gentle and lowly in heart, and you will find *rest* for your souls" (emphasis mine).

This simply means that if we take the low road like Jesus did, all our striving will come to an end. And when we are asked to submit to someone who is younger or to serve others instead of being served, we will find that our hearts will be at peace.

Do you want to be more like Jesus? Look for opportunities to humble yourself.

CHAPTER 13

We Will Be Like Him

I magine with me that someone bought a whole bunch of bright red, crisp apples and tied them onto an apple tree. Everyone who casually walked by the tree would think, *Wow, that tree looks great. See all of those apples?* Unless of course they studied it carefully, they wouldn't notice that the apples were just tied onto the branches. If you let some time go by though, anyone would be able to notice that the now-rotting and sour apples were not really a part of the tree.

Our Christianity can be like that apple tree. By *knowing* the appropriate behaviors, we can make our lives look so spiritual—our praying, our singing, our worshiping and our words. We can become satisfied with simply doing the right things and having the right doctrines. However, here is the problem: You and I can be right in our understanding and all our doctrines, yet be completely wrong on the inside.

Look at the Pharisees. They had everything right. They knew that God is holy. They knew all the laws. They were missionaries. They fasted. They gave. They prayed. They taught the Scriptures.

So what is the problem? Everything began and ended with them. God had no part in it. What God wants us to be goes beyond being right and doing all the right things before man. When you are just performing, Christ is still on the outside. Our "apples" should be produced from the tree. Who we are and what we do must start with the *vine* or our fruit will not last.

Our problem so often is that we want a plan. We want an agenda. We want a book to tell us step 1, 2, 3: "This is how to become godly." But my brothers and sisters, godliness is not a list of how-tos; rather, it is the very life of Christ. How do we become godly? *The answer is Jesus.*

Godliness *is not a list of how-tos; rather, it is the very life of* Christ.

One of the senior leaders in our ministry told me about a man who had been aggressively pursuing the Lord over the past decade. This man made this statement: "All I want is to know Jesus. If someone comes and arrests me, puts me in jail, beats me or kills me, I have no problem. In all this, all I'm longing for is to know Jesus. He is the only thing that matters in my life."

If we listen closely, we'll hear the Lord calling out to our hearts, *Be Mine. Let My life be yours.*

Please, don't look for a quick fix. This call from the Lord is a daily walking with Him, being sensitive to Him, seeking to hear His voice, seeking to do His will, wanting to please Him, loving Him through our choices. It is not obedience to the letter of the law but rather understanding the heart of our Master and making that our very life. This is not a fill-in-the-blank test, but a life consumed with Him, His thoughts, His wishes. It is a nonstop, living, alive, growing relationship with the Creator of this world.

My brothers and sisters, we must see Jesus—everywhere, in all of our life, in everything. Hebrews tells us, "Let us fix our eyes on Jesus" (Hebrews 12:2, NIV).

Have you ever studied a car that was passing you, and all of a sudden without realizing it, you actually started to steer toward the passing car? The more you dwell on negative things, the more negative you become. The more you dwell on positive thoughts, the more positive you become. The more time you spend with someone, the more you actually take on their mannerisms and vocabulary without even trying.

We are called to be partakers of His nature (see 2 Peter 1:4). How do we do that? *We see Jesus.* Scripture says that when we see Him, we will be like Him (see 1 John 3:2). Just like the passing car, the thoughts we entertain, and the people we spend time with—if we look at Jesus and keep Him before us, we *will* go to Him. We *will* become like Him. The measure in which we're able to see Him continually in all our circumstances, in the same measure we will experience Him and His life through us.

In my own life, there was a particular time when I was going through great difficulty. In the midst of that season, the Lord asked me the question: "Are you willing to give up your reputation?" Then I said to myself, *Oh my goodness! He is the One who didn't care what people thought about Him. He didn't defend Himself when people said all kinds of evil about Him. He's asking me if I'm willing to identify with Him and have His nature in me.* And I said back to Him, "Lord, I didn't see this before. I'm happy to do it." Then I was able to find such peace and release from my personal anguish.

Look for Him in your own situations that you are facing right now. Listen to the things He speaks to your heart. Look at His life on earth and consider what it was like for Him. Look for Him in His Word. If we see Him in every part of our lives, we will become like Him.

We will have His attitude toward the Father that says: "I do nothing of Myself" (John 8:28) and "I say whatever the Father tells me to say" (John 12:50, NLT). We will walk in the humility that yields our rights for others and is respectful toward those He created. We'll have His mind to suffer and not be fearful of it. We will manifest His passion to seek and save the lost.

If you have ever read books by Madame Guyon, Andrew Murray, Amy Carmichael, Brother Lawrence, John Hyde, Bakht Singh or Sadu Sundar Singh, you'll find people marked by the nature of Christ. What they write is not just doctrines and theses. Their writings are magnets that pull us to Jesus. There is something about their life so sweet, so precious, so gentle, so humble, so other world. And our hearts in turn say, *I want to be like this person.* They are saturated with the aroma of the gentle, meek, victorious Jesus.

This is the kind of life Christ wants for us. It is a journey. We won't get there tomorrow or the next, but each day as we see Him, we will become more like Him.

Will you seek Him out today? He promises that you will find Him.

CHAPTER 14

A Heart That's Tender

Y<ou know one of the hardest things I have to deal with is to sit in front of a man who has done awful, stupid things in his life or ministry yet has no conviction of sin. Even if he is caught, he acts as if there is no problem and simply asks for a transfer. I am weary of it."

These were the exact words to me from a minister whose denomination appointed him as a counselor for its ministers and church workers across several nations.

Many respected Christian agencies report record attrition rates of up to 80 percent for their well-trained, postgraduate field workers. Most barely survive their second term, and only a few make it past their third. The number-one reason for leaving the mission field is not death threats from an anti-Christian community or lack of funds, but personal relationship conflicts. They simply can't get along with their co-workers or the leadership.

Recent studies have estimated the divorce rate among born-again Christians in America to be anywhere from 35 percent to as high as 72.5 percent. Incidentally, the likelihood of divorce appears to be identical for both believers and nonbelievers. Most couples file for divorce not because of a spouse's infidelity, but because of incompatibility. Again, it's a relationship problem that destroys the foundation of our families and fills our prisons with delinquent teenagers.

Because these reports are not about secular society but represent the condition of the Church at large, we must ask ourselves: *What's wrong with our hearts that we would produce such a poor testimony?*

It seems our hearts are no longer tender toward our God, toward our brothers and sisters in Christ or toward our spouses and families. At the center of each of these relationship problems is our unwillingness to humble ourselves and take responsibility for our sin. Instead, we fight and manipulate others to protect our self-image.

> *At the center of each of these relationship* **problems** *is our* **unwillingness to humble** *ourselves and take responsibility for our sin.*

The phrase "I have sinned against you with my words, attitude or response" comes only with great difficulty over our lips. We find it much easier to say, "I just made a dumb mistake . . . forget it."

What's missing in our so-called repentance is the deep sorrow the prodigal son had when he realized how much he had hurt the heart of his father. This sorrow caused him to lay aside all pretense and self-protection and then to confess with a broken heart, "Father, I have sinned against heaven and in your sight" (Luke 15:21).

Several leaders from a mission field I was visiting approached me with the urgent request to help them make peace between two co-workers. I agreed to talk with both men. The interesting thing was that neither one was willing to give in and admit any wrong. I realized that, technically, the brother who was the leader was absolutely right in what he had said and done. If he took his case to a court of law anywhere in the world, he would be vindicated as innocent. But if he was so right, why was the other brother so hurt? Why did he continue to insist he had been wronged?

Finally I spoke to the leader.

"I understand what you said to this brother," I told him. "But tell me, in what spirit did you speak those words?"

There was dead silence. Then he responded: "I understand what you mean."

Even truth can divide and destroy if it is not soaked and covered in love, grace and mercy—and presented with a tender heart.

If that tenderness of heart is missing in our relationships with our brothers and sisters, God's work is greatly hindered. For Jesus said, "If two of you agree on earth concerning anything that they ask, it will be done for them by My Father in heaven" (Matthew 18:19). With these words, the Lord clearly identified the foundation of prayer: oneness in relationship with each other.

Before going to the cross, Jesus prayed His incredible prayer on our behalf recorded in the Gospel of John. His main petition was "that they all may be one" (John 17:21).

But how is this oneness possible? Will it happen if we all think the same thoughts and, as a result, respond to one another with great kindness, love and understanding? And can we achieve these same thoughts by some deeper-level education that eliminates all differences between us and causes us to live above such things?

You already know the answer.

Humanly speaking, that is impossible. Even in a small local fellowship, the believers come from different family backgrounds and upbringings. All have different personalities, behavior patterns, levels of education and spiritual understanding.

However, one key to love, unity and following the Lord is my willingness to take responsibility for my sin. When my heart is tender before God, I will no longer accuse my brother or sister for my failure.

Instead, I will say, like the prodigal son, "Father, I have sinned." And that attitude will open the way for God to unite us as His people and fulfill His promises. Blaming others became part of our human nature with the fall of man. Imagine this: While Adam and Eve were sinless, they daily walked hand in hand with the Almighty, who dwells in light no man can approach.

But when they sinned, everything changed. God came to Adam and asked, "What on earth have you done?" and Adam answered, "Me? I didn't do it. If You want to know the real problem, it's this woman You gave me" (see Genesis 3:9–12).

Here God had just caught Adam red-handed. The man stood there totally naked, except for a withering fig leaf. He had just lost everything, yet he was unwilling to admit his sin. Instead, he protected and defended himself and shifted the blame to his wife.

And then when God questioned Eve, she responded,

"Well, what can I say? The serpent deceived me" (Genesis 3:13, paraphrased). There will never be unity or rivers of living water flowing through our lives until we come to a place where we take responsibility for our sin.

The thief on the cross experienced this truth in the last minutes of his life when he said, "I deserve this punishment for what I have done." And Jesus immediately responded, "Today you will be with Me in Paradise" (Luke 23:43).

Unity only happens when we yield our rights and admit our failures. If we desire the oneness with our brothers and sisters for which Jesus prayed, then keeping a tender heart is not simply an option, but it is our highest priority.

Whom does the Lord want you to talk to? Don't put off His best for your life.

CHAPTER 15

Which Road Will You Travel On?

Ｗe live in a culture in which, unless we consciously and deliberately seek to swim against the current, we will hardly make it as followers of Christ . . . at least, not the Christ of the New Testament, who said, "And whoever does not bear his cross and come after Me cannot be My disciple" (Luke 14:27).

The Church at large has adapted to the trends of the culture. Frequently the Christian message is presented in a way that caters to people's perceived needs and their desire for an easier, better life. Man and his comfort have become the main focus, and God is obligated to meet these expectations.

This has created a generation of Christians who know little or nothing of sacrifice, suffering and self-denial for the sake of Jesus. We have become conditioned to always seek for a soft cushion, at the least a thin one, if we are asked to sit on a hard bench. Even in the work of God, we avoid difficult tasks, and we question anything that demands physical and emotional discomfort or spiritual battles.

This is in sharp contrast to Jesus, who rebuked Peter for counseling Him not to go to Jerusalem to suffer and die, and later for trying to rescue Him with his sword in Gethsemane. Commanding Peter to put his sword away, Jesus said, "Shall I not drink the cup which My Father has given Me?" (John 18:11).

Jesus was the Lamb slain before the foundation of the world, and He came to suffer and die for our sins. Knowing His purpose and submitting to the Father's will, He chose the hard road, the one that led to Calvary.

> ～ *Submitting to the Father's will,*
> *He chose the* **hard road,**
> *the one that led to Calvary.* ～

Christ set an example for those who followed Him then and for all who want to follow Him now. He said, "Where I am, there My servant will be also" (John 12:26).

You see, God is also asking us to do hard things. For example, Jesus said, "If anyone comes to Me and does not hate his father and mother, wife and children, brothers and sisters, yes, and his own life also, he cannot be My disciple" (Luke 14:26).

God is telling us there is a choice left before us. We have to make a decision between the hard road on which God asks us to go or the easy road everyone else travels.

For Noah, preaching 120 years without results meant choosing the hard road year after year.

Nehemiah, building the wall of Jerusalem, faced constant harassment by enemies from within and without. The easy road would have been to quit, to go back to Persia and live at the king's palace in peace. But he chose the hard road because he was not seeking his own, but the things of God.

We cannot honestly, authentically, reasonably and deliberately serve our Lord without our willingness to accept difficulties and inconveniences—the hard road.

Consider some of the stories of national missionaries in our ministry: two brothers who became porters, carrying heavy loads in a Nepali mountain region in order to win a tribe to Jesus . . . a young man from Myanmar, who walked 17 days through the jungle to get to Bible school, leaving his family behind . . . Bible school graduates who have made the slums their mission field.

Why are they choosing such difficulties? They are following in the footsteps of a Savior who didn't hesitate to lay down His life for a lost world.

Amy Carmichael, pioneer missionary to India, wrote a poem that is actually a prayer. In it, she asks for nothing less than deliverance from her self-seeking nature so that she may serve Jesus freely and totally.

From prayer that asks that I may be
Sheltered from winds that beat on Thee,
From fearing when I should aspire,
From faltering when I should climb higher,
From silken self, O Captain, free
Thy soldier who would follow Thee.

From subtle love of softened things,
From easy choices, weakenings,
(Not thus are spirits fortified,
Not this way went the Crucified)
From all that dims Thy Calvary,
O Lamb of God, deliver me.

> *Give me the love that leads the way,*
> *The faith that nothing can dismay,*
> *The hope no disappointments tire,*
> *The passion that will burn like fire;*
> *Let me not sink to be a clod;*
> *Make me Thy fuel, Flame of God.*[1]

If there is anything that is holding you back from giving your all to Jesus, following Him and choosing the hard road, you need to start calling out to the Lord for His help just as Amy Carmichael did.

Freely give it to Him.

CHAPTER 16

Finding God's Heart

O nce I watched a program on which a reporter interviewed passersby on a busy city street, asking each one the same question: "How can someone get forgiveness of sin and receive salvation?" You wouldn't believe the answers people gave just off the cuff. Most of them spoke totally out of their vivid imaginations.

The Bible has very definite and unchanging answers to these crucial issues. However, it seems people either don't know the Word of God or they just prefer their own opinions on the subject.

Unfortunately, this attitude is not just confined to those who don't know the Lord! Multitudes of believers cling to their own ideas when it comes to serving the Lord and exercising faith.

But this is of huge consequence. God cannot bless us, change our circumstances, heal our bodies, fulfill His promises or put His stamp of approval on our service to Him until we align our thinking with His thinking.

We can mark it down—God will wait and work with us until we change and come to a place where we abandon our own ways of thinking and accept His. However, we can only accept His ways if we know what they are. It takes us deliberately seeking to understand God's *heart* through the passages we read in His Word.

⌇ *God cannot* bless *us until we align our thinking with* His thinking. ⌇

Let's look, for example, at the church of Ephesus in the book of Revelation.

On his second missionary journey, the Apostle Paul preached the Gospel in this city. Incredible miracles happened, and many who received Christ publicly confessed their sins and burned a mountain of costly witchcraft books. The believers born out of this mighty move of God suffered severe persecution and became known for their great love for Jesus, their perseverance and their hard work.

By all New Testament standards, they were far ahead of most of us, especially in the areas of love, dedication and spiritual discernment.

But as time went by, they became cold in their hearts toward the Lord. And we read in Revelation 2:4–5 these frightening words of warning from the lips of Jesus, the Head of the Church: "I have this against you, that you have left your first love. Remember therefore from where you have fallen; repent and do the first works, or else I will come to you quickly and remove your lampstand from its place—unless you repent."

If we are honest, it looks rather unfair to us that Jesus threatens to put the light out in this exemplary church. Why would He want to burn the whole barn down for one small rat? After all, this church in Ephesus had 99 things right and only one thing wrong.

What, then, is God's real reason behind pronouncing such a severe judgment? God's heart concerning work, sacrifice and service sharply differs from ours.

To God, everything we live, say or do as believers is valued by the underlying motive found in our hearts. When He looked upon the situation in Ephesus, He saw that the reason for their faithful service had changed. Their true motivation was no longer love, but duty. For them, the visible service had become most important, but for God, it was the internal condition that counted.

God saw an empty shell void of the wonderful life the church of Ephesus once had, and He was going to remove their lampstand. Yet in His mercy, He revealed to them His thoughts and showed them the way to recover their loss: *Repent and do the first works.*

Outwardly they didn't have to change anything, for they had always practiced the first works. But inwardly they needed to give up their own ideas about what successful ministry was all about. They had to realize that it was not work and more work, but loving the Lord—and then serving Him motivated by this overflowing love in their hearts.

The Lord knows that we so easily impress ourselves by the outward appearance of our accomplishments for Him: the hours we spend in prayer, the knowledge we acquire about spiritual things, the money we give for Christian causes, the position we hold at church or in a ministry and the number of people we teach or to whom we witness.

I believe the Lord wants us to examine closely the reason

why we do all these wonderful things. After all, like the Ephesians, we also could end up building a structure made of wood, hay and stubble (see 1 Corinthians 3:10–15).

What, then, is the only safe measuring scale for our work for the Lord? It is finding God's heart about our service for Him—as revealed in His Word. His thoughts should permeate every aspect of our lives. God does not want us just to change our behaviors, but our very being. As we change our heart to His, He will change our attitudes, our actions and our very lives. Our life will then bring forth lasting fruit.

Today, seek to know your Lord's heart.

CHAPTER 17

Neither Do I Condemn You

James and John were furious. These Samaritans had the gall to close their village to Jesus just because He was traveling to Jerusalem. Instead of being overwhelmed with gratitude that the Jewish Messiah would even set foot on their soil, they closed their doors.

Convinced that these heathens didn't deserve another breath, the two disciples volunteered to call fire down from heaven, like Elijah, and wipe them out. Jesus rebuked them immediately with these words: "You do not know what manner of spirit you are of" (Luke 9:55).

Jesus' closest followers reverted to serious carnality just days before His crucifixion. This incident tells us something. In our own selves, when we are rejected or mistreated, we are capable of forgetting all the spiritual things we have learned and responding with judgment and retaliation just like the rest of mankind.

What happens to us that we so quickly look down on others? Along with Jesus' disciples, we as believers sometimes feel we are qualified and even called to judge others because we think we know the laws of God and are zealous for righteousness.

But Jesus didn't judge those Samaritans who rejected Him. Neither did He judge the prostitutes, sinners and tax collectors who came to listen to His sermons.

The religious leaders brought Jesus a woman caught in adultery, convinced they had Him trapped. He was a Jew. He knew the Law of Moses. The stones were ready—He would have to pronounce the death penalty over her. But when He challenged those who were without sin to cast the first stone, one by one they left, each convicted by his own failures.

In the end, Jesus, the one and only One who could have passed judgment over her, sent her away with the words, "Neither do I condemn you; go and sin no more" (John 8:11).

What prevented Jesus from judging others? It was His knowledge of the purpose for which His Father had sent Him to this earth: "For the Son of Man did not come to destroy men's lives but to save them" (Luke 9:56), and "He has sent Me to heal the brokenhearted, to proclaim liberty to the captives" (Luke 4:18).

Unless we learn to leave judgment to God, we act like a wrecking crew, demolishing lives wherever we go, and do not exhibit the Spirit of Christ.

I remember a massive old building in downtown Dallas, which I passed every day as I went to seminary. But one day, to my surprise, the entire building was gone. I learned that a demolition crew had brought it down within seconds. All that remained was a huge pile of debris, which trucks were in the process of hauling away.

This is a very vivid picture of what happens when we begin to judge others. Unlike our Heavenly Father, who looks upon the heart, we only consider the outward appearance. That's the reason we end up misjudging people's motives and having no mercy for those who fail.

For the same reason, Eli, the priest who was supposed to represent God's heart, looked at Hannah in her agony and thought she was drunk. And no one but Jesus noticed the enormous sacrifice the widow made when she put her two coins in the offering box at the temple.

Matthew 7:1–5 clearly tells us not to judge because we are not qualified nor called to do so. The consequences of not staying within our job description are much more serious than we think. First of all, we will be judged with the same measure that we use to judge others. But also when we judge, we inflict additional wounds on those whom the Lord seeks to make whole and set free.

God wants us to walk through this world with great spiritual sensitivity and discernment. We should not think that He wants us to close our eyes to unrighteousness. However, instead of judging, He has given us a ministry of compassion.

> *While the whole world was condemning One, that* One *was hanging on the cross for the* whole world.

While the whole world was condemning One, that One was hanging on the cross for the whole world. Failure and weakness in others' lives should only make us aware of their needs. It should evoke compassion in us and a desire to bring healing and wholeness to their lives. It should lead us to pray and cooperate with God's work in them.

Thus, instead of judging and destroying, we become agents of change. We respond as Christ did and in obedience to Him who has asked us to follow His example.

What is your default: judgment or compassion?

CHAPTER 18

Christ, Our Identity

Has it ever sunk into your heart that Jesus and you belong to the same family? You are even named after Him. And "Christian" is not just your new family name; it's your whole identity.

God wants you to know what this means because it will anchor your Christian walk and give you inner strength, freedom, confidence and clear direction.

It's essential that we find our identity in what God declares about us in His Word. Let's make His proclamations personal. I encourage you to continue the list I've started here:

I am a child of God (see Romans 8:16).
I am a conqueror through Him (see Romans 8:37).
I am an ambassador for Christ (see 2 Corinthians 5:20).
I am His witness (see Acts 1:8).

Because God wants all of us to be His witnesses and ambassadors while we live on earth, each of us has a special role in His kingdom. Perhaps we are called to be a Barnabas, an encourager; a Timothy, who faithfully serves and learns under an older servant of God; or a Stephen, who is a fearless witness. Know God's call on *your* life. Write it down. It's important for you to know where you fit in God's plan.

When we study the lives of those in the Bible whom God called for a specific purpose, we often find that many gained clarity regarding their identity and mission while going through trials and wilderness experiences.

> ❧ *Many gained clarity regarding their* identity *and mission while going* through trials *and wilderness experiences.* ❧

Jacob, after 20 years of scheming and failures, finally came to the end of himself. In the midst of all hopelessness, he heard the words from the Man who wrestled with him all night: "Your name shall no longer be called Jacob, but Israel" (Genesis 32:28). Jacob understood his identity was no longer that of a deceiver but that of a prince. From that moment on, his life changed until it matched what God said about him.

After 40 long years living as a refugee and shepherd in the wilderness, Moses had even lost his ability to articulate well. That's when God told him, "I will send you to Pharaoh that you may bring My people, the children of Israel, out of Egypt" (Exodus 3:10). Moses' identity in God's plan was that of a deliverer who knew God face-to-face. This became clear to him after all the glamour of Egypt had been stripped away and he stood alone in the wilderness before the burning bush. As he began to walk in his identity, Moses fulfilled God's plan.

Gideon, hiding and scared to death of Israel's enemies, heard the Angel of the Lord declaring his identity to him: "The LORD is with you, you mighty man of valor!" (Judges 6:12). He first thought it was a bad joke. However, each time Gideon stepped out on this declaration with a tiny bit of faith, he found it to be true, and he increasingly gained courage. In the end, we see him boldly marching with 300 people against an enemy "as numerous as locusts" — and God giving him the victory (see Judges 7:12–8:12).

Even Jesus spent 40 days in the wilderness, fasting, praying and facing severe temptations, before He started His public ministry. Although He already knew who His real Father was, He revealed His identity as Messiah only after His wilderness experience.

None of us looks forward to facing difficulties, loneliness, misunderstandings, problems and accusations. All these can present real wilderness experiences. I want to encourage you not to let these times be an end in themselves, but to find in them who you are in God's plan.

Being aware of who we are in God's kingdom is important for our stability on this journey. Every day Jesus encountered people who publicly declared that He couldn't be the Messiah. Even His closest followers were oftentimes confused about His identity.

How did He ignore all those voices around Him and continue His journey toward the cross without being shaken? He listened to and believed only one voice — that of His Father. Each time people asked Him who He was, He confessed the identity His Father declared about Him.

We must follow the footsteps of our Lord. We too must refuse to give in to the voices of our mind and emotions and whatever negative things other people tell us. Instead, we must confess, believe and act upon the identity Jesus gave us in His Word and the calling of God upon our lives. This will lay a strong foundation for our life and service to God and set us free to live through Christ.

Whose voice will you believe?

CHAPTER 19

Free to Make Progress

I was stunned and amazed to no end when I read the 19-page letter a man wrote me. He not only blamed me for all the mess he had made of his life, but he also pronounced severe judgment and terrible curses on me from God and the devil.

Never in my life had I received anything so full of poisonous hatred. The most incredible thing was that I had never met the man in my life. I had no clue of the situation to which he referred.

Because he had the audacity to make me responsible for all his tragedies and setbacks, I sat down to write him a fitting defense to his wild accusations. But just as I finished, I asked myself, "What am I doing?" I tore up my letter and threw it away.

> No one on earth can destroy you, not even God; only you can destroy yourself.

Then I took an aerogram and wrote him a one-sentence reply: "My dear brother, no one on earth can destroy you, not even God; only you can destroy yourself."

You see, the man's real problem was that he never searched his own heart for the root cause of his crisis. Instead, he believed that if I straightened up, his problem would go away, and he would be happy and successful in his endeavors.

This man is certainly not alone in thinking he can blame people around him for his lack of success, peace, comfort, happiness or spirituality. That's why a husband looks for his wife to change and a wife wants her husband to shape up.

Wanting to feel good and grow spiritually by changing everybody else becomes a vicious cycle. We are convinced that our progress depends on their compliance. We seldom stop and honestly look at ourselves.

It is true that others can be a source of trials, disappointment and challenge, but we cannot blame them for our own lack of spiritual vitality. That's a matter of our heart and not of outward circumstances.

In fact, throughout Christian history, those believers who went through immense trials, horrendous persecution and martyrdom were the very ones who carried the Christian faith forward. They gained their spiritual strength and endurance in the midst of adversity, and their faith was refined as gold through fire. In order to grow spiritually and become faithful until death, they did not depend on people around them to change. Even in chains, they were free to make progress in pursuing God.

The truth is that no one person can hinder our spiritual growth or destroy us if we walk with the Lord and put our faith in Him. He will be our shield and defender just as He promised. Even God cannot destroy us, if we have trusted in Jesus as our Savior and our hearts are completely His. He will eternally abide by His own Word that says, "Whoever believes in Him should not perish but have everlasting life" (John 3:16).

Ultimately, I am the only one who can destroy me. By my own choice to reject Jesus as my Savior, I can send myself to hell. As a follower of Christ, if I violate God's principles, I will bring destruction upon my marriage, my home, my work and myself. And if I don't walk by faith according to the Scripture, I can prevent God from fulfilling His promises toward me.

How can we detect the *real* hindrance and remove it? The Apostle Paul advised the Corinthian Christians to examine and judge themselves (see 1 Corinthians 11:31–32). It starts with us being willing to be honest with ourselves. Instead of blaming others, we should search our own hearts when we find that we are not making progress in our Christian walk.

But it shouldn't end there because "the heart is deceitful above all things, and desperately wicked; who can know it? I, the LORD, search the heart, I test the mind . . ." (Jeremiah 17:9–10). Our hearts can appear innocent to us so that we don't suspect our troubles could be self-inflicted.

We must involve the Lord on this quest. We must be willing to be honest with ourselves and then invite God: "Search me, O God, and know my heart; try me, and know my anxieties; and see if there is any wicked way in me, and lead me in the way everlasting" (Psalm 139:23–24). Only He can tell us the truth and help us see ourselves as we are. That's why each of us needs to follow David's example— coming in humility to the Lord and asking Him to perform the examination.

God was always faithful to point out a sin or a wrong attitude in David's heart that compromised his relationship with God and hindered his spiritual progress. David responded by humbling himself, repenting and accepting God's correction.

It is the grace of God when He opens our eyes and shows us our true condition. And if we respond as David did, the hindrance that held us back will be gone, and we will be set free to make progress on our spiritual journey.

Lord, search our hearts and try us.

CHAPTER 20

What's the "One Thing"?

T wo individuals came to Jesus, each with a deep spiritual problem. One found life, but the other lost it. What went wrong in this counseling session?

The first person was a rich young ruler who approached the Lord with the most burning question of his heart: "What shall I do to inherit eternal life?" (Luke 18:18).

He was not seeking a religious debate as so many others did. He honestly wanted to know. When Jesus listed five of the commandments, the young man replied that he had a perfect record in keeping them all. Christ simply responded to him, "You still lack one thing. Sell all that you have and distribute to the poor . . . and come, follow Me" (Luke 18:22). Scripture tells us that the rich ruler went away sorrowful (see Matthew 19:22).

The second man was also rich, but he had gained his wealth by shamelessly defrauding others. Zacchaeus was a well-known crook. When Jesus came to his house, He said nothing to the man about selling his house or giving his money away. Amazingly, Zacchaeus freely made the decision to give half of his possessions to the poor and restore four times the amount he stole to everyone he'd cheated.

What was it that compelled Zacchaeus to respond so differently than the rich young ruler?

When Zacchaeus saw Christ, he saw the pearl of great price. He saw in Him everything, all things, completion. He realized, *If I have Him, I can easily give away everything. What else do I need?*

But when the young ruler saw Jesus, he didn't see the pearl of great price. If we could know what his thoughts were that day, I imagine most of them were focused on what he would be giving up, more than what he would gain in Christ.

We very often make the same mistake as the rich young ruler. We truly want to follow Christ and experience His abundant life, but we focus on what we may have to give up and are afraid to let go of those things we have relied on for so long.

I believe the Lord looks for that "one thing" we grasp so tightly and depend on. It could be anything: our strength, our abilities, our education, a meaningful relationship, our years of Christian experience, our connections, the good reputation we have established, our position, our extraordinary discernment and other spiritual gifts, our plans for marriage or the things of this world like the rich young ruler.

In the New Testament book of Revelation, we encounter a group of people in the church of Laodicea who were convinced that they were rich and lacked nothing. Yet the Lord told them that they were wretched, miserable, poor, blind and naked. Why did the Lord think they lacked everything? It is because they had become self-reliant, which prevented them from experiencing the genuine life of Christ.

As long as we hold on to that one thing in which we

trust, we will never be able to surrender fully to Christ. Consequently, there will always be a distance between the Lord and us. Such lack of closeness results in frustration and discouragement on our part. In addition, that one thing will be a constant hindrance for the rivers of living water to flow freely out from us and give life to others.

How do we recognize the "one thing" still lacking in us? We will know it by the discouragement, tension, bitterness, frustration and irritation that fill our hearts, when that "one thing" is tampered with. God will open our eyes, and we will recognize it if we truly desire to. We will then have the grace to surrender it to the Lord, not by looking at what we are letting go, *but* by looking at all that we have in Christ— the pearl of great price.

You see, if "our riches," that which we value most, are the Lord and what we have in Him, then no raging storm can cause any disturbance. Amy Carmichael once wrote, "A cup brimful of sweet water cannot spill even one drop of bitter water, however suddenly jolted."[1]

If "our **riches**,*" that which we value most, are the* **Lord** *and what we have in Him, then no raging storm can cause any disturbance.*

I believe the Lord wants us to live in a continual state of seeing Him as everything and being content in Him alone. Those whose life is full of joy and the unhindered presence of the Lord are the ones who experience a continuous feast on Him. Nothing else will matter to them, and abandonment to Christ alone is their obvious choice.

Will you believe that He is truly the pearl of great price? Step out. You'll find Him to be so much more than you imagine.

CHAPTER 21

The Mark of Humility

Two men went to the temple to approach God in prayer and seek His favor. One, a Pharisee very sure of his outstanding spiritual achievements, recounted to God his flawless service record. He even thanked the Lord that he was better than others, especially that tax gatherer over there. This other man didn't dare lift his head. He stood at a distance and pleaded guilty as a sinner, asking God for mercy (see Luke 18:9–14).

It is obvious that the Pharisee, though his outward behaviors may have looked good, was full of pride. And in contrast, the tax collector was quite aware of his unworthiness and was sincerely humble.

It is important to note: *Lack of humility is the proof of counterfeit spirituality.* The Pharisee thought he had everything so right, but his "spirituality" was not authentic. So many people have so many things to say about the Lord and their walk, but there is a sense that there is nothing *real* in the spiritual life they're portraying. The mark of humility is missing. True spiritual maturity will be marked with humility. After 20 years of preaching and a life of hardship and sacrifice, Paul said with a sincere heart, "I am the chief of sinners" (see 1 Timothy 1:15).

Having that mark of humility is God's plan for all of us as believers. But often we all still experience a lack of respect and love for mankind. We can be insensitive to people's feelings and indifferent to their circumstances. It can show up as hidden anger, impatience, irritation, bitterness and a tendency to quickly pass judgment. If we analyze these feelings and actions, we find that all of them have their roots in pride. Like the Pharisee in Jesus' story, we feel superior in some area, and we aren't able to manifest the long-suffering love of Christ in our relationships.

In contrast, Christ dealt with people in humility. During His earthly life, He sought to lift others up, even when He confronted them with their problems. He never looked for opportunities to gain a higher position, more respect or greater honor for Himself. That's why He could tell His disciples to follow His example and be servants of all, to choose the last seat instead of the first and most prestigious.

~♀ *Jesus* never *looked for opportunities to gain a* higher *position, more respect or greater honor for Himself.* ♀~

We cannot manufacture humility. The moment someone *tries* to be humble, we notice it like a bad taste in our mouth. The outside actions may look right, but their spirit doesn't match. Humility manifests itself from the reality and understanding we have within us. Natural man with all his knowledge and determination cannot simply be humble.

Christ is our answer. He must be our focus. It is Him working within us and us responding to Him by which we will truly become humble. When we humble ourselves before Him and desire His work in this area, He has the open door to work with us. And He will.

Then in our relationships with others and our daily events of life, we will have many chances to humble ourselves in response to His promptings. Each of these moments is an opportunity for us to be conformed into the humility of Christ and have that mark of humility on our lives.

James 4:10 exhorts us: "Humble yourselves in the sight of the Lord." For our transformation into Christlikeness, this is where it starts. Will you make a commitment today to practice this Scripture? You will find that your love and compassion for others will grow tremendously, and you will experience the joy of being a servant like Jesus.

Don't wait.

CHAPTER 22

Choosing Not to Return

After we are saved and begin our relationship with God, we learn that our journey with Him has just started. We discover every day that the ordinary components of life—relationships, emotional security, accomplishments, our profession or position, financial stability or even our cultural or national heritage—can hinder us from fully giving our lives for His purposes and growing closer to Him. One by one, God calls us to walk away from these things.

Abraham, Moses and Joseph—all those in the "cloud of witnesses" who have gone before us—were also called to walk away from their "normal" lives (see Hebrews 11:4–12:1). Let us see how they responded:

> All these people . . . admitted that they were aliens and strangers on earth. People who say such things show that they are looking for a country of their own. If they had been thinking of the country they had left, they would have had opportunity to return. Instead, they were longing for a better country—a heavenly one. Therefore God is not ashamed to be called their God, for he has prepared a city for them (Hebrews 11:13–16, NIV).

The "opportunity to return"—what a significant phrase this is!

It is a challenge to follow His call to walk away from these things—but it is an even greater challenge to realize we always have the chance to turn around, to go back to a life that is more comfortable.

Our Enemy, the devil, knows this, and he works hard to persuade us to do so. Let us look at what he uses to try to make us return:

Material things. Demas, one of Paul's co-workers, had this problem. This man traveled so many miles with Paul and shared hardships with him; he could have become another Timothy, but Paul says of him, "Demas has forsaken me, having loved this present world" (2 Timothy 4:10). We will face financial struggles of some sort, have friends who are better off than we are, and feel the need to do something to improve our lives or take better care of our families. The devil will use this. It's a strong pull, but we must make the decision: *Life or death, we will not return.*

> *We must make the decision:*
> *Life or death, we will* **not return.**

The fear of the unknown. The children of Israel suffered under terrible slavery in Egypt. Yet after God led them out and did mighty acts on their behalf, they longed to return, remembering the leeks and the garlic. What happened? They were afraid of what would happen to them in an unfamiliar land filled with giants. We, too, face unknowns; what we must remember is that God is bigger than the giants, our problems and our fears.

Losing our focus and vision. Paul's earthly journey was marked by his passion to know the Lord intimately. He said he counted everything as a loss compared to knowing Christ (see Philippians 3:8). Those in the cloud of witnesses had one thing on their mind—their desire to be in heaven with the Lord. Our aim is the Lord Himself. Hebrews says, "Let us fix our eyes on Jesus" (Hebrews 12:2, NIV).

And out of that pursuit of Him, who first loved us, comes a heart to reach the lost. Jesus came to seek and save the lost (see Luke 19:10). And as we grow to know Him more, what is important to Him becomes important to us. Out of Paul's pursuit of the Lord came an undying passion for the lost. He was constrained by his love for Christ to live a life of incredible suffering, from which many heard the Good News (see 2 Corinthians 5:13–14, KJV).

Paul kept his focus and was able to say near the end of his life, "I have finished the race" (2 Timothy 4:7). You and I will stay faithful to continue on this journey as long as we keep the end in mind. Don't let the devil use day-to-day discouragements to take you off course.

Spiritual deception. So many Christians lose sight of God's call when they become ensnared in self-focus and introspection—all in the name of godliness, deeper life and devotion.

Only one theme runs through the entire Bible: Christ, the Savior of the world. The Old Testament promises the coming of the Redeemer. The four Gospels narrate the fulfillment of Old Testament promises through Jesus' birth, death and resurrection, thus completing the work of redemption. The book of Acts is the account of those who knew Jesus as Lord as they went about preaching the Good News of Christ throughout the whole world. The Epistles instruct believers on living and demonstrating Christ's life to the world. And the book of Revelation is the final chapter in which we, the redeemed, will meet at the Marriage Supper of the Lamb and will be with Him forever and ever.

Knowing Christ and walking intimately with Him will produce a love and passion for the lost world. In more than 40 years of serving the Lord, I have found that the more I get to know the Lord, the more concern I have for the lost. It is no longer about the need, but it is for the Lord's sake. If our so-called "deeper life" doesn't have this result, it is a counterfeit and a distraction.

So as we face the pull of this world and the pressure from the devil to walk away from God's call, let us remember that we are on earth for only a short time. We are strangers and aliens to this world. We only have a visa for this life, but our passport is from another country.

The men and women of Hebrews chose not to return to their earthly country because they recognized that God's work went beyond time and space. Their true country was a heavenly one. May the Lord find us, too, focused on what is real and authentic—beyond circumstances, what we feel, what others say or what the Enemy throws at us. And if He were to write another chapter like Hebrews 11, may He use your name and mine as examples there for others to follow.

This world is not our home—let us journey toward that eternal city.

CHAPTER 23

Not at the Finish Line Yet

M any years ago I was invited to speak to a group of medical doctors who were interested in missions. I was excited to share with them about the lost world—until I walked into one of their homes where the meeting took place.

To my mind, the house was nothing less than a king's palace. I was so angry and upset that I spent half of my speaking time attacking materialism. Anyone who heard me could clearly understand that I was condemning the brother who owned the house.

Would Christ have done this? I think not. I should have used all my time to cry out for the lost world and ask for prayer.

It seems that all of us, as believers, have our own paradigms, views and convictions. Many of them are the result of God's dealings with us in certain areas of our lives or His gracious opening of our understanding to His Word. But somehow we forget the time and effort it took for the Holy Spirit to bring us to that point, and we begin to judge others by the light we have received.

When others fail or act outside our convictions, some

automatic mechanism seems to go off inside us. Unless we are careful, we will judge others without mercy.

Even the Apostle Paul failed in this area when he was dealing with John Mark. This young man had left Paul's team perhaps because things got rough on their first missionary journey. In his zeal and absolute commitment to Christ, Paul had no room for someone who didn't share his radical lifestyle and willingness to sacrifice all for the sake of the Gospel. Later, when John Mark asked for a second chance, Paul's reaction, I am sure, damaged the hope of this young brother (see Acts 15:36–39).

While Jesus was with the Father, He watched Abraham trying to substitute Ishmael for the promised son, Moses killing the Egyptian, Ruth the Moabitess worshiping idols and David committing adultery and murder. But from eternity past, He could see their entire life—past, present and future—all at the same time. He knew that by the time they reached the end of their lives, each of these people would be counted among the heroes of faith.

I believe one of the reasons Jesus didn't judge others during His time on earth was because He remembered that the final stretch of their race was still ahead of them. They hadn't crossed the finish line yet, and between now and then, much could still change.

Jesus knew that Peter's denial and Thomas's doubting of His resurrection were not the last chapters in their apostleship. He could see when both of them would lay down their lives as bold witnesses and martyrs for the Gospel. In the eyes of God, it's the final moment, the way we cross the finish line, that counts.

Isaiah 42:3 says this about the Lord: "A bruised reed He

will not break, and smoking flax He will not quench." His goal is never to finish us off but to help us succeed. That's our calling as well.

> *The next time we are tempted to judge others, let us* remember *that the* final chapter *of their life has yet to be written.*

The next time we are tempted to judge others, let us remember that the final chapter of their life has yet to be written. How we treat them may be a part of their story to victory.

Will you be one on their rescue team?

CHAPTER 24

Small Beginnings

U zziah must have been trembling with fear when he was made king over Judah after his father's death. Although the royal crown was sitting on his head, he was just a 16-year-old kid who didn't know what to do with life, much less with leading a nation.

But in his ignorance and confusion, Uzziah had one good thing going for him. He was humble enough to cry out to the Lord for guidance: "He sought God . . . and as long as he sought the Lord, God made him prosper" (2 Chronicles 26:5).

We are also told that "he was marvelously helped till he became strong" (2 Chronicles 26:15). Because of his humility and dependency on the Lord, this inexperienced young king made the right decisions and soon became mighty and famous.

Over the years, however, a significant change took place in Uzziah's heart that caused him to lose everything he ever possessed—including his life. "But when he was strong his heart was lifted up, to his destruction" (2 Chronicles 26:16). In violation of God's laws and despite the warning of the priests, he entered the temple to burn incense and was struck with leprosy right in front of the altar.

The sudden judgment that came over Uzziah certainly makes his story stand out in the Bible. But more than that, it's a very serious warning to each of us. We must guard our hearts so they will not drift from humility, end up in pride and ultimately cause our own destruction.

> ~ We must **guard** our hearts
> so they will not drift from humility,
> end up in **pride** and ultimately cause
> our own **destruction**. ~

Remembering a few Christian organizations whose journeys resembled Uzziah's, one of my staff members once asked me, "Do you think this could happen to Gospel for Asia?"

My answer was very, very long, but I began with, "If we forget our beginning . . ."

I have no doubt that every believer, servant of God, church and ministry will sooner or later face the strong temptation and opportunity to move away from humility and walk in pride. Oh, it may just be a mere sense of self-accomplishment, undetected by those around them, but it will be obvious to God, who knows the secrets of our hearts.

God is aware of how easily our hearts become lifted up in pride; that's why He often reminded the children of Israel to look back to the pit from which they had been dug out (see Deuteronomy 32:10; Isaiah 51:1; Hosea 2:1).

From my own short journey in serving the Lord, I do not know anything more destructive and damning than individuals who have forgotten how they first came into the Lord's work.

It was God who raised them up and gave them a message and voice to be heard, along with access to thousands of people and resources. It was God who provided co-workers, secretaries, telephones, computers, emails, airplane tickets, platforms from which to speak, microphones, radio stations and TV cameras.

But after a while, they somehow began to forget the pit, the dirt and the muck from which they were pulled. And now, like Uzziah, all of a sudden they say or think in their hearts, *Oh yeah, I was 16, and I didn't know what to do. But then I learned my way quite fast, and I made it.*

When Uzziah was judged with leprosy, we read some very strange words. No one kicked him out of the temple. He hurried out himself. You see, during all the years when he was humble, the grace of God covered and protected him each time he came into the Lord's presence. But now his pride had caused him to walk out from under God's grace. This is the most dangerous thing anyone can do, because once God's grace is removed, we inevitably encounter His righteous judgment that gives us exactly what we deserve.

May we never forget that God always resists the proud and gives grace to the humble (see James 4:6).

In my garage, I keep an old, scratched-up hollow door that I bought for a few dollars from a lumberyard 30 years ago. Laid across two sawhorses, it served as my first official desk for Gospel for Asia. This old door helps me remember our small beginnings and that it was surely God's grace that has brought us to where we are today.

Remember the place from which God has taken you.

CHAPTER 25

The Weapon of Disunity

At the end of a devastating three-year drought, all Israel assembled at Mount Carmel. There Elijah boldly challenged them to watch a contest between the prophets of Baal and himself.

After the prophets of Baal exhausted themselves in vain to persuade their god to answer by fire, it was Elijah's turn to call upon Jehovah.

But before he did, he first rebuilt the altar of the God of Israel: "And he repaired the altar of the LORD that was broken down. And Elijah took twelve stones, according to the number of the tribes of the sons of Jacob . . ." (1 Kings 18:30–31).

This act of Elijah is of great significance. These 12 stones speak of the unity that was required before he—or anyone else—could see God's work accomplished. Then Elijah could only go as far as two sentences into his prayer before the fire of the Lord fell and consumed the sacrifice, the wood, the stones, the dust and the water in the trenches.

Jesus' disciples might have felt small compared to the mighty prophet Elijah. However, Jesus told them how they could have the same presence of God and experience His powerful answers to their prayers: *by being united in their hearts.* "If two of you agree on earth concerning anything that they ask, it will be done for them by My Father in heaven. For where two or three are gathered together in My name, I am there in the midst of them" (Matthew 18:19–20).

I hope that you will not miss the seriousness here. The work of God goes forward through unity. Without it, what happens to God's purposes here on earth? Consider this quote from Paul Billheimer's book *Love Covers:*

> The most important, momentous, crucial, but the most ignored, neglected and unsolved problem that has faced the Church from its infancy to the present throbbing moment is the problem of disunity. . . . The sin of disunity probably has caused more souls to be lost than all other sins combined. Possibly more than anything else, it is the one thing that binds the hands of the Holy Spirit and thwarts His work of convincing of sin, righteousness and judgment.[1]

Without any doubt, disunity is one of the most powerful weapons Satan uses to hinder the work of God. We should guard against it at all costs.

So often we get caught up in the face value of our lives and situations that we don't even realize how demons are blowing things out of proportion, twisting the facts and manipulating situations all with the aim of creating disunity. Yet when we respond in a godly manner, we thwart Satan's tactics. Christlike attitudes will save us from words and actions that would have caused rifts in the Body of Christ. What are the thoughts and attitudes that keep us from responding in Christlikeness and the spirit of unity?

A judgmental spirit. Having a judgmental spirit means we have a critical and unloving attitude toward others. We think we have the only right answers. We measure everyone and everything by our standards while our critical and unmerciful attitude toward others is just as displeasing to the Lord as the sin we see in them.

Jesus vividly illustrates this contrast by comparing our judgment with that of a man who tried to remove a speck from his brother's eye while having a log in his own. He goes on to tell us that such a self-righteous attitude has severe consequences: "Judge not, that you be not judged. For with what judgment you judge, you will be judged" (Matthew 7:1–2).

Lack of brokenness. Unless we are willing to give up our own ambitions, we cannot be one with the other members of the Body of Christ. If we are so adamant about our rights and our ways, we are not able to live and work together in God's kingdom.

> *As long as we are* unwilling to admit *that we are wrong, we are weak and there is* no unity *among us.*

Each one of us has to come to a place at which we recognize the depths of our self-love and then repent and be willing to say, "I am sorry." As long as we are unwilling to admit that we are wrong, we are weak and there is no unity among us.

Unwillingness to become servants. The Apostle Paul wrote to the Corinthians: "For we preach not ourselves, but Christ

Jesus the Lord; and ourselves your servants for Jesus' sake" (2 Corinthians 4:5, KJV).

Do we serve others because it is convenient or when we know we will be praised? Or will we serve simply because it is our privilege to take a low position?

The way we respond to Christ and humble ourselves before Him is reflected and judged by the way we respond to others around us. Jesus said, "Inasmuch as you did it to one of the least of these My brethren, you did it to Me" (Matthew 25:40).

It's easy to climb up the ladder; the hardest thing is to go down by choice. I believe this is where we are tested—to see if we are willing to humble ourselves and maintain unity by serving others.

Clouded vision. Like soldiers on the battlefield, if we fall down, we continue on. We don't walk out of the battle. When we face difficulties—times of misunderstandings, differing opinions, disappointment or missed expectations—our vision can become clouded, and we forget the war that is raging.

But Paul urges us, "Stand fast in one spirit, with one mind striving together for the faith of the gospel" (Philippians 1:27). We are in a battle for souls, and our unity is so crucial to accomplishing this purpose. So don't let the times of difficulty blur your vision. Remember why you were enlisted.

The destiny of nearly 3 billion unreached people hangs in the balance. Yet not a day goes by that we don't hear of disunity in the Body of Christ, whether it's among individuals, denominations or mission groups. So often division takes place over such small issues that are not at all crucial in order to maintain fellowship in Christ. Do you know how splintered we are? We are one Body, one Church, yet we have more than 3,000 different denominations.

My dear brothers and sisters, we cannot afford to be playing games. May the Lord give us the courage, clear thinking and brokenness to walk together in unity.

Will you lay down your own agenda for the sake of the many who are waiting to hear the name of Christ?

CHAPTER 26

Act on God's Word

Peter risked becoming the joke of his hometown when he rowed out in broad daylight to the deep waters of Lake Gennesaret and let down his net to catch fish. Everyone watching him from the shore must have thought he'd gone mad. Even a small child could have told him that if he wanted to catch fish, he must do it at night and in shallow water.

But this was a moment in Peter's life when he did the right thing first. He had just listened to Jesus teaching the multitudes from his boat. It must have touched the heart of this fisherman so deeply that he was willing to forsake all his professional expertise and go about fishing in all the "wrong" ways, just because Jesus told him to do so.

He could have politely said to Jesus, "I respect You for being a great teacher and an excellent carpenter, but believe me, Your knowledge about fishing is really off. Take it from an expert—what You suggest will never work."

Instead, Peter replied, "Master, we have toiled all night and caught nothing; nevertheless at Your word I will let down the net" (Luke 5:5).

That day Peter discovered that when he abandoned his

own thoughts and acted on God's Word and God's thoughts, he experienced a wonderful miracle.

I am often amazed when I read in the Gospels how the experts in the law of Moses—the Pharisees and Sadducees—rarely, if ever, experienced miracles in their lives. At the same time, common people who knew very little—Peter, the Roman centurion whose slave was sick and the widow whose only son had died—witnessed the most incredible wonders. Surely these theologians in Jesus' time had sickness and urgent needs in their families just like everyone else. What prevented them from seeing God's promises fulfilled?

I believe it was pride causing them to cling to their own clever thoughts. Pride wouldn't allow them to humbly acknowledge that they could be wrong and that God's thoughts and ways were so much higher than their own.

By the way, we see the same thing happen in our day as well. Young national missionaries and simple believers on the mission fields of Asia experience a book-of-Acts-type of Christianity on a daily basis, whereas many of us "Bible experts" seem to miss out.

You see, the foundation for learning to walk with the Lord, for serving Him and for becoming a blessing to others begins with the humility to act on God's thoughts instead of our own.

The foundation for learning to walk with the Lord begins with the humility *to act on* God's thoughts *instead of our own.*

Peter, the centurion and the widow (like those simple believers on the mission field) had nothing to hold on to. Unlike those religious leaders, they were not preoccupied with protecting their reputations or guarding traditions and someone's teaching. That's why God's Word could flow freely into their lives and become the basis of their thoughts and faith and, in turn, their actions.

We too must come to God with the same humility and submission, telling Him: "Lord, I don't know; I want to learn; I want to change."

And, by the way, we cannot use psychology, carnal reasoning or philosophy to bring about these changes—to pull down wrong thoughts, imaginations and anything that causes us heartache and cripples our faith.

God's Word clearly says that this very real battle has to be fought with spiritual weapons: "For the weapons of our warfare are not carnal but mighty in God for pulling down strongholds, casting down arguments and every high thing that exalts itself against the knowledge of God, bringing every thought into captivity to the obedience of Christ" (2 Corinthians 10:4–5).

The most important factor in abandoning our thoughts is to look in the Bible and see what God says about a matter. Then we must determine to act on His Word rather than on our own thoughts or those the devil may whisper into our minds.

For example: If I think, "No one loves me," God's thoughts on the same subject are, "I have loved you with an everlasting love" (Jeremiah 31:3).

If I say to myself, "I failed," God's Word says to me, "For whatever is born of God overcomes the world" (1 John 5:4).

If my thoughts are, "I am weak," the Lord says, "Let the weak say, 'I am strong' " (Joel 3:10).

If I am convinced that "I can't do it," God's truth is that "I can do all things through Christ who strengthens me" (Philippians 4:13).

How can you learn to apply God's promises to your life and in turn experience His blessings? When you face troubles, problems or uncertainties and you don't know what to do next—stop for a second. Ask yourself: *Am I thinking the thoughts of God? Am I doing what the Lord would do in this situation? Am I making the decision? What does the Lord say about this? How can I respond to it?*

If you don't know the answer, go to your Bible. Check your concordance or ask someone to help you find God's thoughts concerning your problem. See if you can find an example in God's Word in which someone faced a similar situation.

Then pray over the Scripture portions you find. As you do, the Lord will enlighten you. The verses will no longer be abstract to you but instead will become living words for your situation.

Put your life in the context of Scripture. Start thinking God's thoughts about your situation and act on them in faith. As you daily practice and develop this habit of applying God's promises, it will become second nature as you grow in following the Lord.

Abandoning our thoughts and humbly taking God's thoughts as our own truly honors Him and revolutionizes our faith.

Start acting on God's Word today. Don't delay.

CHAPTER 27

God Watches Out for Us

I t was fall while I was visiting Germany. Rev. Wolfgang
Mueller, our senior leader there, took me for an after-
noon ride in his car to show me the breathtaking coun-
tryside.

The weather was beautiful, the air was crisp, and many
trees were loaded with fruit nearly ready for harvest.

As we were driving along, we passed by an apple orchard. I was amazed at the enormous amount of fruit each
tree carried. But to my bewilderment, many of those trees
had collapsed, limbs and branches were broken off, and the
fruit was rolling on the ground.

Brother Wolfgang stopped the car, and we both just
looked at the tragedy. There must have been hundreds of
apples on each of those tree branches; but now, because
they were broken off, none of the fruit would ever reach
harvest time.

"This is really bad," I said. "What happened?" Rev.
Wolfgang answered simply, "The owner didn't take care of
these branches."

Then he drove on and showed me another orchard.
These trees were as huge as the first ones, and their branches

bore even more apples. But strangely, none of the trees had collapsed, and not even a single branch had broken off.

What made the difference? The owner had carefully put wooden props under each branch to help carry and support the tremendous weight of the fruit.

This memory is forever etched in my mind, and God used it to teach me an important truth.

John 15 teaches us that Jesus is the vine, and we are the branches. God prunes us countless times. Throughout this process, our character has become more Christlike, and we have gained a deeper understanding of the Lord and His Word. We are no longer the kind of person we were 5 or 10 years ago.

God is then able to entrust us with greater responsibilities and more fruit. When this happens, God in His care puts a support under our branch to prevent it from breaking off. But God's support for our branch is not joy, peace, acclamation or the applause of men we might hope to receive. It is instead pain, trials and difficulties—something God chooses in His wisdom to keep us from getting proud and not being able to support the weight of the fruit.

> ~⚬ *God* chooses *in His wisdom to*
> keep us *from getting proud.* ⚬~

Look at the Apostle Paul. He came to a point in his life when he could say, "Imitate me, just as I also imitate Christ" (1 Corinthians 11:1). His character was so transformed and his life was bearing so much fruit that God could entrust him with tremendous insight and revelation. But strangely, at the same time, the Lord also appointed a thorn in the flesh to bother him. Paul thought it was a hindrance to his ministry, and he prayed three times for God to remove it.

But God didn't grant his request. Instead, He told Paul that His strength was made perfect in Paul's weakness. The thorn in the flesh kept him from pride and arrogance in his insight and accomplishments. God was saying, "The revelations I gave you are so high and you bear so much fruit that your branch needs My strength to support it; otherwise, it will break off."

The moment Paul understood that this thorn was not his enemy but rather his support, he said *yes* to it and was grateful that God was watching out for him.

As an expression of His love for us, God seeks to support us in all that He's called us to do. He ensures that our inner life keeps pace with the task He has assigned to us, for unless He "supports" us, we would become proud and arrogant. Ultimately, He prevents us from becoming spiritual casualties. As a good gardener, He watches out for us!

Say *yes* to the support He lovingly sends your way.

Chapter 28

Expand Your Borders

"KEEP OUT" – "Genius at work, don't disturb" – "Knock before you enter" – "Don't touch" – "Private supply" – "Don't bother me" —these are just a few examples of the signs you can pick up at the store to hang on your doorknob.

Some of them are illustrated with intriguing pictures, but they all convey the same message: "This is my world. Respect it, or I will treat you as an intruder."

We live in a culture in which we are raised and taught to be independent, private and protective of our personal rights, space, time and comforts. Others should not cross the line we draw around ourselves or encroach upon our personal world. We are not thrilled when others interrupt or disturb our own pursuits with their concerns and problems.

The Lord, instead, tells us: "Be merciful, just as your Father also is merciful" (Luke 6:36) and "As the elect of God, holy and beloved, put on tender mercies . . ." (Colossians 3:12).

Whenever close family members of mine travel to places that could be potentially unsafe, I think about them and pray for their safety with much compassion and deep concern. I am involved in their trip with my whole heart—my thoughts, emotions and imagination. And I am ready to help in any way I can.

Generally, we are prepared to show this type of compassion to our immediate family and close friends when they are sick, hurting or in danger. We take the interruption into our personal life in stride during their time of need.

But what about those outside our small circle? When new families join our growing church or ministry, do we expand our feelings of closeness and relationship to include them?

And what about those farther away: national missionaries who suffer persecution while preaching the Gospel . . . the Bible school student who was tortured by his relatives and barely escaped with his life . . . the teenage girl who received Christ and whose parents beat her daily, made her sleep outside the house and told her that she was no longer their daughter? Should we feel compassion toward these as well, even if we have never met them personally? Is it not enough if we stick with our efforts toward our own families?

Speaking of family, Jesus, our brother and Lord, clearly defined for us who our family members are: "For whoever does the will of God is My brother and My sister and mother" (Mark 3:35).

This means that those suffering missionaries are my brothers and sisters; the Bible school student who barely escaped with his life is my son; and the teenage girl living on the street—rejected and forsaken by all—is my daughter.

The Lord wants us to expand our borders. He wants to weep, touch, feel, pray, fast and show compassion through us to more than just our close circle of friends and family. As believers, we have given Him our lives, which include our hearts, minds, mouths, ears, eyes, hands, feet and everything we are. Though He has bought us with a heavy price, we may have not consciously surrendered all these aspects of our lives to His leading.

The Lord wants to show compassion **through us** *to more than just our close circle of friends and family.*

Instead of being totally available to Him, we can often find ourselves self-centered, calloused and disconnected toward the crises we hear about. How do we transition to the place at which the Lord's heart of compassion flows through us freely?

Before the inception of this ministry, my heart had become cold, and I found I was more concerned about the small things in my life than I was about the lost world. That's when I desperately prayed: "God, You have to change me; I cannot change on my own." And by His grace, He began to break my heart and make it tender and compassionate toward others.

If you hunger to have the Lord's compassion flow through your life, I encourage you to ask God to do for you just what He did for me. I am confident He will.

However, I want you to know that He will bring you to a place at which you must die to your own self, your freedom and your attitude of self-preservation. One book that greatly helped along this line and taught me to understand how to love others is *The Calvary Road* by Roy Hession.[1]

God not only wants us to expand our capacity of love

and compassion to the rest of the Body of Christ but to the lost world as well. We must continually let His heart flow through us; otherwise, we will not be able to embrace even one additional person or maintain the increased number of our relationships. For this reason, we must constantly yield our hearts to Him so that He can continue to break them and fill them with genuine compassion toward others.

In my own life journey, one of the things I pray on a regular basis is, "Lord, always keep my heart soft." There is a Scripture in Job 23:16 that says, "For God maketh my heart soft" (KJV). The Lord is more than willing to accomplish this in each one of us.

God, break our hearts with the things that break Your heart.

CHAPTER 29

Choose Humility

There was a time in my life when I would become quite impatient with others when they couldn't discern things that were obvious to me regarding people, circumstances, ministries or decisions to be made.

I would think ugly words such as: *How dumb can you be? Can't you see this? What's wrong with you? Two plus two is four. What does it take for you to see this?* I would go on and on in my head, and my emotions would get all charged up.

By God's grace, He didn't kill me. Instead, He slowly began to show me my heart of pride. It was as if the Lord said, "You see, it was I who freely gave you the grace, gifts, abilities, discernment, understanding and skills you possess. But now you are using them to beat up on others, and you condemn, criticize and put them down. Do you want Me to allow you to become a vegetable, lying in your bed, unable to talk or move around?"

It was a frightening thought to entertain, and I knew all it would take was a car accident. This rebuke from the Lord made me realize that my worst enemy is not the devil, but my own selfishness and lack of humility.

Look at King Nebuchadnezzar, King Uzziah, King Saul.

Some of them started so well. But once their hearts were lifted up, they fell just like it says in the book of Proverbs: "Pride goes before destruction, and a haughty spirit before a fall" (Proverbs 16:18). If a time comes that we say like the Laodiceans, "We are rich, we are able, we got it made and we don't need anything," then the Lord will say back to us, "You are wretched, miserable, poor, blind, and naked" (see Revelation 3:17). *God opposes the proud* (see James 4:6, NIV). This statement from God's Word should cause us to be sober.

My worst enemy is not the devil, but my own selfishness and lack of humility.

Why is pride so damning? Why is pride so dangerous?

Pride will not allow us to love others. In Luke 15, the older brother of the prodigal son was so proud of his responsible behavior and hard work that he had no compassion or love left for his younger brother. In fact, because he saw himself as so much more important and superior, before his father he no longer referred to him as "brother," but rather "this son of yours" (Luke 15:30).

Paul exhorted us in Philippians 2:3: "In lowliness of mind let each esteem others better than himself." There is no way we can have a heart of love and respect for someone, genuinely regarding them as better than ourselves, as long as there is pride in us and we feel that we are above others!

Pride seeks for man's honor and for position, no matter what. We will even use our worship and service to God to achieve this goal. That's why Jesus warns us: "Take heed that you do not do your charitable deeds before men, to be seen by them . . . as the hypocrites do . . . that they may have glory from men" (Matthew 6:1–2). For what purpose do we seek this glory? Does it bring honor to the Lord?

We can no longer see our own faults or sin. Pride blinds us. The Pharisee standing in the temple next to the tax gatherer prayed, "God, I thank You that I am not like other men . . . or even as this tax collector" (Luke 18:11). Jesus called the Pharisees blind leaders of the blind (see Matthew 15:14). We will not be able to accurately see ourselves, others or even God when we are trapped in pride.

It is obvious that the right choice for our lives is to choose humility. Who wants to reap the consequences that the path of pride will yield?

The question is: *How can we maintain a life of humility?* The answer is simple. There is only one medicine for all sicknesses caused by our pride: *Follow Jesus.* He is our life and our example in all things. Instead of striving to figure out how to respond to a situation, the best we can do is to choose to follow Him.

We will find that Jesus chose to serve instead of demanding to be served. He instructed His disciples: "If I then, your Lord and Teacher, have washed your feet, you also ought to wash one another's feet" (John 13:14).

Giving up all His own ideas, Jesus saw all things from the Father's point of view: "Shall I not drink the cup which My Father has given Me?" (John 18:11).

And He lived in total obedience to His Father, regardless of the cost to Himself: "And being found in appearance as a man, He humbled Himself and became obedient to the point of death, even the death of the cross" (Philippians 2:8).

As long as we continue to "let this mind be in you which was also in Christ Jesus" (Philippians 2:5), we will maintain lives of humility that God will honor and bless.

Choose to have this mindset of Christ.

CHAPTER 30

With Each Stroke of the Brush

Have you ever watched an artist paint a picture at a street corner or in a park?

When the artist first takes his canvas, puts it on the easel, dips his brush into a color and begins to paint, he alone knows how the painting will look when it is completed. For me as a bystander, it's a complete mystery. I may even wonder what on earth he is doing. But slowly the painting emerges—with each stroke of the brush. Finally, I stand amazed before a marvelous picture, and now that I can see the end result, everything the painter did along the way makes sense.

Did you know that God is such an artist?

All of humanity, the sons and daughters of Adam, sinned and became by choice slaves of Lucifer. Controlled by demons and totally darkened in their spirits, they agonized and fought but could not escape the grip of darkness and Satan's kingdom.

When Christ finally came on the scene, He overcame our Enemy through His death on the cross and destroyed him who had the power of death (see Hebrews 2:14). In Christ, we who were destined for hell were forever set free and translated from this horrible kingdom of darkness into the kingdom of God's dear Son.

In Ephesians chapter 1, Paul reveals that our redemption through the precious blood of Jesus is only the beginning of what God has in mind for His Church (see Ephesians 1:7–8). If indeed our salvation, forgiveness of sin and deliverance from hell were all God had planned for us, then it would have been best if He had taken us to heaven right after we were born again. That way, we would no longer have to live on this sin-ridden and temptation-filled earth. But God left us here.

What exactly is God trying to do? We find the answer in Ephesians 2:10: "For we are His workmanship, created in Christ Jesus for good works, which God prepared before-hand that we should walk in them."

Some years ago, I completed a detailed study on the book of Ephesians. It was an exhilarating experience for me when I looked up the word "workmanship" in the original text. I discovered the Greek word used is *poiema*, from which we derive the word "poem." It means "handiwork" or "craftsmanship."

This verse describes God as a poet or an artist at work on His masterpiece. Deep within the heart of God is an ache to see the work completed. He sees every brush stroke it will take, and His heart is filled with emotion as He brings it to pass.

As children of God, we are His painting, His poem, the expression of His heart in our generation. Romans 8:29 tells us: "For whom He foreknew, He also predestined to be con-formed to the image of His Son." This simply means that we are predestined for this one purpose: to become like the Lord Jesus Christ.

The goal of God, the Master Painter, is that with each stroke of His brush, the life, character and nature of Jesus increasingly fill our hearts and are clearly expressed through us.

As children of God, we are the **expression** *of His heart in our generation.*

As we allow ourselves to be transformed into the image of Christ, we are able to represent Him to our generation, to serve others with His love and compassion and to have rivers of living water flow from our lives to a lost and dying world.

May this song written by Albert Orsborn become the desire and prayer of our hearts:

> *Let the beauty of Jesus be seen in me,*
> *All His wonderful passion and purity;*
> *Oh Thou, Spirit divine, all my nature refine*
> *Till the beauty of Jesus be seen in me.*[1]

When He finishes with His painting, we will see the expression of the Master Designer in a life fashioned after the likeness of Christ.

Trust Him with His masterpiece—let the beauty of Christ be seen in you.

CHAPTER 31

It Takes Time

O ne of the struggles we sometimes face as followers
of Christ is seeing where we want to be in our walk
with God in contrast with where we currently find
ourselves.

There are all kinds of reminders around us to tell us of
our fallen nature and the spiritual maturity we have not yet
attained. The Enemy is an accuser of the brethren, and he
actively takes every opportunity he can to accuse us (see
Revelation 12:10). His accusations leave us despairing and
hopeless. Sometimes we just don't want to try anymore, and
we are ready to give up.

If we turn to Christ in those times instead of lingering
on the Enemy's words to us, we'll hear another story. Christ
causes us to look up and to stop thinking of ourselves. He
draws us to repentance and encourages us to believe Him
for a greater work through our lives. With Him, there is
hope and a brighter tomorrow.

When we are confronted with our failures, it's important that we realize the process of becoming like Christ
takes *time*. There is no microwave for godliness. It takes
years upon years of patient, hopeful perseverance. As we

let Him live through us—one day, one moment, one choice at a time—we are becoming more like Christ, a little more today than we were yesterday.

What happens to us when we don't realize that this is a long-term journey?

The first obvious implication is that we are impatient and frustrated with ourselves. And then if we don't realize the foolishness of our "instant Christianity," we'll try our own quick fix. We'll simply try to "act" our way to the godliness we want. Or we'll make a "plan of achievement." Often people think that knowledge is what they lack. If they only "knew" more, they would perform better.

But all these attempts of the flesh play right into the Enemy's hands. Others sense our hypocrisy, as we do ourselves, and we can't help but loathe it. "Our plans" to be better, if initiated in our flesh, either end in failure and more discouragement or in success and pride. And knowledge itself will not produce godliness. It can actually puff up or discourage us if it's not what God has for us in our current season.

The fact is that none of these responses draws us any closer to our original goal of becoming more like Jesus. They all lead us into the Enemy's trap—*thinking about ourselves continually.* There is no faster way to sink into the pit of despair than to spend all our time thinking about ourselves and how we're not measuring up. We'll end up at a buffet of self-pity, condemnation and an equally critical spirit toward others.

So what's our answer? Believe that the Lord *will* complete us.

We must cling to the reality that God is doing His work in our lives (see Philippians 2:13) and stand on His promise

138

that "He who has begun a good work in you will complete it until the day of Jesus Christ" (Philippians 1:6).

Jesus embodied this for us in His life on earth. He lived for 30 years under the authority of His parents before beginning His ministry. The Bible tells us that "though He was a Son, yet He learned obedience by the things which He suffered" (Hebrews 5:8). Day by day, Christ chose to die to Himself, to say *no* to His own will and *yes* to His Father's will. He needed that length of time to grow in obedience and come to the point at which He would choose absolute surrender—surrender to the point of death on the cross.

Let us also have patience—with ourselves as well as with others. God is much more concerned about our honesty before Him and our attitude of grace and mercy toward others than He is about us doing everything correctly.

> *God is much more concerned about our* **honesty before Him** *and our attitude of grace and mercy toward others than He is about us doing everything correctly.*

So let us remember: It takes time for God to do His work. We do not have to lose heart because of any spiritual lack we discover in ourselves.

"Commit your way to the LORD," Psalm 37:5 encourages us. "Trust also in Him, and He shall bring it to pass." The Almighty God is at work in our lives. We can certainly trust Him for the journey He has set for us!

He *is* completing His work in you. Believe Him!

CHAPTER 32

Destroying Deception

In *The Silver Chair*, one of the books in the Chronicles of Narnia series, author C.S. Lewis vividly illustrates what happens when someone falls under deception.

Prince Rilian, the king's son and heir to the throne of Narnia, is held captive by the enchantments of a wicked witch who poses as a beautiful and kind lady. He can't remember who he is and where he came from. For 10 long years, he has lived in the witch's castle, not recognizing that she has made him her slave. In fact, he thinks she is his greatest benefactor and gladly obeys her wishes and counsel.

Each night, there is an hour during which his mind experiences flashes of memory from his real past. However, the witch convinces the prince that during those times a spell turns him into a vicious and murderous serpent. To protect him and others, she graciously provides a magic silver chair that she claims will eventually break the spell. Believing her words, the prince allows himself to be tied to this chair every night until the dreadful hour passes.

The real truth is that the witch's sorcery weakens each night. The prince could regain his identity and complete freedom were it not for the silver chair that once again reinforces the power of the enchantment.[1]

It is possible for us as Christians to lose touch with our true identity—if Satan succeeds in deceiving us!

> *There is no greater threat*
> *to Satan's kingdom than Christians*
> *who know and* live *their identity* as sons
> *and daughters of Almighty God.*

There is no greater threat to Satan's kingdom than Christians who know and live their identity as sons and daughters of Almighty God. Satan is unable to stop or defeat such followers of Christ, unless he succeeds in stealing their knowledge of who they are in Him.

How does he do it? Through lies and deception.

The Lord Jesus tells us about Satan's tactics and his nature:

> "He was a murderer from the beginning, and does not stand in the truth, because there is no truth in him. When he speaks a lie, he speaks from his own resources, for he is a liar and the father of it. . . . The thief does not come except to steal, and to kill, and to destroy" (John 8:44, 10:10).

For example, when a believer sins in any way, Satan immediately whispers to his or her mind: "Even if God forgave you, you will never recover from what you have done; God has laid you aside; you are a disgrace."

If the believer is not firmly grounded in the Word of God and does not reject the Enemy's words, those whispered lies would plunge him into a vicious cycle of deception. He would no longer see himself as a conqueror and ambassador for Christ but would assume the false identity the devil gave him and live in it.

The tragic thing is that a person who is deceived does not know it. Like Prince Rilian, he will believe a lie to be the truth and subject himself to actions that only strengthen his bondage and deepen his imprisonment. In the case of a believer who loses his identity as an overcomer, each time he meditates on his failure, he reinforces the deception that God can no longer use him.

The only way to recognize deception is by the un-Christlike fruit it produces in our lives. We are discouraged and live with self-condemnation, the past haunts us, our inner strength wanes, our hope diminishes and problems seem to be invincible mountains. Our estimation of ourselves is that we can't make it, and we become spiritually paralyzed.

All this is exactly what Satan is after. He knows he can't take us to hell, so he deceives us to make us ineffective and fruitless for the kingdom of God.

What we must do is call out to the Lord and then do what Prince Rilian did: He took up his sword and destroyed the silver chair.

In our case, we must take up the sword of the Spirit, which is the Word of God. With it, we destroy every one of our imaginations and the lies of the devil that are contrary to what the Bible says about our identity as Christians. The Apostle Paul instructed us to do this: "For the weapons of our warfare are not carnal but mighty in God for pulling down strongholds, casting down arguments and every high thing that exalts itself against the knowledge of God, bringing every thought into captivity to the obedience of Christ" (2 Corinthians 10:4–5).

This will set us free once again—free from the deceptive words of the Enemy and free to follow Christ as He called us to.

Get your verses ready and don't let the Enemy keep you bound!

CHAPTER 33

The Power of Oneness

I t didn't take very long after the flood for Noah's descendants to act independently from the Living God and band together to construct the Tower of Babel. When the Lord came down to inspect their ambitious and idolatrous building project, He made a very serious statement that teaches us volumes about oneness: "Indeed the people are one and they all have one language, and this is what they begin to do; now nothing that they propose to do will be withheld from them" (Genesis 11:6).

These words reveal the incredible power that is found in unity, even if it is used for an evil reason.

We have seen the truth of this Scripture demonstrated over and over throughout history when people rallied around a leader with an ungodly ideology and joined together to spread it by force to the rest of mankind.

But the good news is that this power of oneness is equally true when we as believers unite together in doing God's will: *Nothing will be impossible for us.*

Jesus had that total oneness of spirit with His Father. That's why everything God wanted to do through His Son here on earth was fulfilled—unhindered. What was the key to such unity? *It was the love they had for one another.*

Think for a second how you take care of yourself. You won't get a hammer and bring it down on your thumb. You won't deliberately hurt yourself. Obviously, you care about what happens to you. When we truly love one another, what affects someone else, affects us. We won't do something to deliberately hurt someone else. We *want* them to do well even if they've hurt us deeply. Jesus desires this kind of oneness in His Body. It far supersedes any unity the world could produce for its cause.

The devil knows this fact well, and he is afraid of the damage his own kingdom would suffer should God's people succeed in becoming one in spirit. That's why he fights so very hard to divide the Body of Christ and to keep believers from loving each other.

In fact, whenever God does something significant through His people, the most likely—and severe—counterattack will come in the area of unity, specifically broken relationships.

Nehemiah's biggest problem in rebuilding the wall of Jerusalem was not the outside enemies who were trying to kill the Jews, but rather disunity among his own people. Instead of giving themselves to one another and to the building project, they were trying to bring division. Nehemiah had to spend crucial time sorting out problems and rebuking with painful words the very people he had come to help.

In the New Testament, much of the Apostle Paul's energy was consumed in dealing with divisions within churches and between individuals.

In his first letter to the Corinthian believers, he addresses their selfish conduct during the Lord's Supper, which he pointed out was a clear indication of disunity—that they didn't discern the Body of Christ, the Bride of Jesus. Paul warned them that their self-centeredness and lack of love for each other were bringing them judgment (see 1 Corinthians 11:17–22).

The Lord's primary goal in any local fellowship is for all His people whom He placed there to sincerely love and care for one another, producing such oneness that His purposes can be fulfilled through their lives. In fact, Jesus told His disciples in John 13:34–35 that this would be the key to conquering the world with the Gospel: "A new commandment I give to you, that you love one another; as I have loved you, that you also love one another. By this all will know that you are My disciples, if you have love for one another."

> ~*The Lord's primary goal in any local fellowship is for all His people whom He placed there to* sincerely love *and care for one another, producing such* oneness. ~

May the Lord challenge our hearts afresh and cause us to reexamine ourselves that we not be unloving toward anyone. Let us be people who will choose to go down and take that extra step to care for others and demonstrate Christ's love to them. When we do this, we will make it obvious that we are His disciples, and He will draw this world to Himself.

Whom would God have you become more loving toward?

CHAPTER 34

I Choose . . .
That Others Might Live

When Jesus came to live on this earth, He entered a world in which everyone continually fought to preserve his or her own rights, reputation and life. How foreign it must have sounded to them when Jesus, in reference to the cross, replied to those who wanted to see Him:

> "The hour has come that the Son of Man should be glorified. Most assuredly, I say to you, unless a grain of wheat falls into the ground and dies, it remains alone; but if it dies, it produces much grain. He who loves his life will lose it, and he who hates his life in this world will keep it for eternal life" (John 12:23–25).

In this Scripture, Jesus talked about the prospect of a single seed producing many more of its kind. But the most important requirement for that single seed to multiply is this: It must fall into the ground and *die*.

In Mark 4, Jesus told the parable of the sower who went out to sow seed. Some of his seed fell on the wayside, some on the rocky ground, others among thorns and the rest on the good ground. Now just suppose the seeds that fell on the good ground didn't actually die. How much harvest would they have produced? None! In fact, there would have been no difference, in terms of the end result, between these seeds and the ones that fell on bad soil.

Think about it. You can take the best seed and put it in the best soil, but if it will not crack open and die, what good is it?

With a grain of wheat, Jesus illustrated how very serious a matter it is that He and we, His followers, die in order to produce life. Even if we had every doctrine right, lived our lives beyond reproach and could move mountains by our faith, it would be insufficient to produce life in others. Without death there is no harvest.

Jesus, being 100 percent God, could have decided to lay down all His glory, become a man and later on go back to heaven . . . alone. But He saw that through death, He would bring many sons to glory. Out of His free choice, He willingly embraced the cross (see John 10:18; Hebrews 2:9–10, 12:2).

So it is with us. Paul wrote, "I die daily" (1 Corinthians 15:31) and "I am crucified with Christ" (Galatians 2:20, kjv). The death he talks about is a continuous present tense. It's a choice I must make every day of my life to die to my own desires, rights, wishes and decisions for the sake of bringing fruit for the kingdom of God. There is no shortcut and no other way.

In the measure in which you and I are willing to die daily through the grace of God and the cross, in that same measure will life be produced in others. Paul put it this way:

"So then death is working in us, but life in you" (2 Corinthians 4:12).

I am sure when Paul finished his race, he looked back on the death that worked in him—the bloody trail of suffering, hardship, loneliness, shipwreck, prison and rejection—and had no regrets. I am sure there was only praise to God who called him (see 2 Corinthians 4:17). He brought many with him to heaven, and even today, after 2,000 years, his choice to die continues to bring fruit through the words he left behind.

In the measure in which you and I are willing to dic daily, *in that same measure will* life be produced *in others.*

What about those of us who believe we must be so private and so protective of our time, energy, resources and reputation in order to further our own spiritual pursuits? You will find that in spite of all the knowledge and blessings accumulated, those lives would remain fruitless. Essentially, all that is happening is self-preservation.

A man who is willing to go the extra mile, carrying the burden for someone else, is at that moment dying to his desire for rest and more peace for himself. He sees the extra mile as a means to help that person see God's love.

Someone who truly understands that death to himself will produce life in others will not watch the clock in his service to the Lord. When there is need, he will work alongside Jesus as long as it takes. He will pray for the lost world while others are sleeping. As he dies to his rights to stop working at 5:00 or to sleep an extra hour, he opens the way for thousands around the world—on the mission field and elsewhere—to find life.

Such a follower of Jesus will not hesitate to humble himself before others when he has failed. He will trust God that through his honesty and willingness to receive correction, life will be produced.

It is true if we superficially look at others who live for themselves, we can become jealous of the so-called "easy" life they live. We can begin to tell ourselves, "I have rights too." The pressure grows especially when our friends, families, the media and churches counsel us contrary to Christ's call to lay down our lives.

Paul said that he had the right to be married, just like Peter and the rest of the apostles. It wasn't wrong; but he chose not to so that he could serve the Lord with undivided attention (see 1 Corinthians 7:7–8).

So the choice we make in dying daily is not between right or wrong. The choice is between my rights and a new way—Christ's way. In other words, when we say no to many things and accept the cross, regardless of how much it hurts, that one seed can give life to hundreds more.

Death to your own wishes will mean life for multiplied others—what will you choose?

CHAPTER 35

A Gospel of Great Joy

When I first saw a few clips from *The Visual Bible's Matthew*,[1] I didn't like it. It showed Jesus laughing, celebrating after healing the sick and throwing children up in the air and catching them. He always seemed to be enthusiastic and happy when He was teaching or dealing with people.

You see, I come from a culture in which spirituality is measured by how solemn, dignified and holy your appearance is. This means that as a servant of God, you must wear white clothes, keep a serious face even if you are happy and carefully guard your behavior. You wouldn't want to spoil your image by laughing out loud or running around playing with the kids.

All this actually comes from eastern mysticism, in which the way to holiness and spirituality is asceticism—the renouncing of all worldly pleasures, comforts and emotions. It is a counterfeit spirituality produced by Satan.

After viewing this film, I read through the four Gospels again just to see what Jesus was really like. For the first time, I gained an awareness of someone who was genuinely happy. There was a spirit of celebration, a positive note that I saw in His life. People felt drawn to Him, and in His presence, those with deadly diseases and even the worst sinners were filled with new hope.

Jesus came to this earth not to add gloom and hopelessness to people's lives, but to bring light, hope, laughter and the joy of heaven to a sin-ridden world.

The angels didn't announce His birth by saying, "Oh, what a sad and gloomy event. God's Son is going to be persecuted and killed. Let us mourn and weep." No! They were praising God and telling the shepherds about the good news of great joy for all people.

Jesus vividly illustrated for us with the parables of the lost coin, sheep and prodigal son how all of heaven breaks out in elaborate celebration over each sinner who turns to God (see Luke 15:7). He even portrays God the Father as the One who initiates the banquet, singing and dancing.

Above all, the joy, happiness and celebration will never come to an end in heaven. Psalm 16:11 says, "In Your presence is fullness of joy; at Your right hand are pleasures forevermore."

What a place that will be!

As believers, we have something outstanding that the world yearns for. Think about it—why do people like to listen to music, watch comedy shows, tell jokes, read cartoons or storybooks and play games? There is something in human nature that longs to smile and be happy. Yet all the happiness the world can offer is short-lived.

Our joy originates from heaven and is therefore able to fill our hearts even in the midst of suffering and difficulties. Paul and Silas, severely beaten and in chains, were celebrating in prison. Why? Their joy was anchored not in their own strength but in the promises of God: that all things would work out for their best, that Jesus had gone to the Father to prepare a place for them and that He would return to take them there.

∿ *Our joy originates from* heaven *and is therefore able to* fill our hearts *even in the midst of suffering and difficulties.* ∾

What about us? Do people encounter that overflowing joy, found in Jesus and the early Christians, in our lives as well?

There is no more powerful advertisement for the reality of the Gospel than a believer filled with the love of Christ and the joy of heaven.

Why is it, then, that our joy is so often nowhere to be found? We allow the problems of this world to overtake our heart and emotions. At the same time, we forget—or simply don't believe—the promises of God that tell us not to be anxious for tomorrow and not to fear because He has overcome the world. We start counting our woes instead of counting our blessings. And we fail to recognize the goodness of God and His encouragement in our surroundings.

To begin to live a life filled with the joy of heaven, we must make a conscious decision to reverse all these trends.

One of the best ways to learn to smile is to go on a "God Hunt," which is how my dear friend David Mains would describe it on his radio program. This simply means that I look every day to discover even the tiniest thing God deliberately arranged in my life to tell me of His love and care:

Perhaps somebody writes a letter, calls on the phone or says a kind word, just when I need it. A motorist stops to let me safely cross the street. Someone offers to carry my grocery bag when I am exhausted. A total stranger smiles at me when I feel gloomy, as if God is reminding me, *Be happy—I am with you.*

Jesus, the One we serve, is the Light of the World. In Him there is no darkness, and there is so much to be happy about as we follow Him. Praise God!

What good things did God do for you today?

CHAPTER 36

Because of Jesus

I had never heard anything like it.

In a village on the Gujarat-Madhya Pradesh border in India, 50 families came to know the Lord within a short period of time. These were very simple but God-fearing people who heard the Gospel and responded to Jesus—Jesus who forgave their sins and set them free from bondage.

In the midst of their celebration and joy, they received an ultimatum. Their village chief and a band of others rounded up these 50 families and told them that they could no longer live in the village.

These new Christians hurried to pack their tattered clothes, pots and pans and other few belongings, and then they walked away from everything they had known. Like refugees from a war zone, they trudged out of the village, along with the elderly who could hardly walk, little children and pregnant women.

As they were leaving, the village chief told them that they would be allowed back only on two conditions: payment of a 500-rupee penalty per family, plus each would have to deny Christ.

But not one of them returned. They walked until they

finally crossed over the border into Madhya Pradesh, finding shelter under trees in the jungle.

I thought about these people and the suffering and hardship they went through just to survive and find a place to settle down. They were so new to the faith. None of them had any theological background or had had a chance to attend seminars, retreats or Bible studies.

They had never even heard about some of the most elementary truths of the Bible, much less complex issues such as eschatology with its pre-, mid- or post-trib viewpoints. I doubt that any of them knew the books of the Bible. In fact, most of them were illiterate.

What made them willing to walk away from their huts, fields, friends and relatives?

If you asked them, this is what they would tell you: "We are walking away because of one reason—Jesus."

What causes a young brother in Maharashtra, India, to decide to return to the same village where he was nearly beaten to death for leading 25 people to Christ?

What gives African Christians in Sudan the endurance not to renounce their faith, but to go through continuous suffering, pain and death?

They all understand what it means when Jesus says: "Follow Me." You see, Christianity is not following a system, theology, doctrines or some ideas. *It is following Him.*

In all things that we do, we must keep in mind that the highest, most sacred call the Lord gave us is to walk with Him, to love Him and to know Him.

That's why Paul wrote to the Philippians: "For to me, to live is Christ, and to die is gain" (Philippians 1:21). In chapter three, he explains the purpose for which he renounced all things—not to reach the whole world with the Gospel, not to become a revolutionary, not to travel all over the world and plant a thousand churches—no, none of those things, but "that I may know Him" (Philippians 3:10).

The highest, most sacred call
the Lord gave us is to walk with Him,
to love Him *and to know Him.*

When we read through the book of Acts and all the letters Paul wrote, we see the result of one man's commitment to know the Lord. Everything Paul did—evangelism, missions, sacrifice, hard work day and night—it all came out of one thing: loving Jesus, knowing the Lord.

Unless our knowledge of the Bible turns into a relationship with Jesus, the strong winds of persecution, discouragement, enticement from the world, a better job, higher salaries, concerns for the future, life struggles and relationship problems will knock us down; we will no longer closely follow the Lord.

There is no doubt that the three Hebrew young men survived the fiery furnace because of their love for the Lord. That's the reason the fourth one, the unseen One, was there with them. And Moses rejected his position in Egypt, for by faith he saw "Him who is invisible" (Hebrews 11:27).

Every individual in the Bible who really came through and was approved by the Lord didn't get there because of his or her achievements. It was because of a close, personal relationship with the Lord. That was the sustaining power.

It takes this kind of love to go through trials and persecution just as those 50 families did who gladly walked away, willing to lose all and live and sleep under some trees in the jungle. Somehow, in their newfound faith, they saw "Him who is invisible" more visibly and tangibly than some of us do, who have learned everything and know our theology inside and out.

Today, the call of Jesus remains fresh and real: "Come, follow Me" (Luke 18:22). His footsteps will take us to the most unreached, to the suffering, to lost and dying millions. But serving them, interceding on their behalf and sacrificing to send missionaries to them will never be a burden for us because it's all for Him. If we truly see the invisible One, all we do is because of Him, and it is truly our privilege and joy.

His arms are open wide—let us run after Him.

CHAPTER 37

Where Is the Master Plan?

D uring the last few days of Jesus' life here on earth, the entire universe, all creation and all the angels in heaven eagerly watched every moment. They didn't want to miss a second! He was the Lamb of God who was slain before the foundations of the world. Thirty-three years ago, they had witnessed in amazement as Jesus stepped out of eternity into time, becoming a human being in order to redeem mankind. Now He was about to wrap up His mission, but it looked as if He were running out of time, with most of His future strategy still to be set up.

First Peter 1:12 tells us that angels actually long to know the details about our salvation. I suppose they had a thousand questions as they watched Jesus walk toward Calvary.

Once in a missions conference, I heard a speaker detail a possible conversation between one of these curious angels and Jesus. It went something like this:

Angel: Jesus, could You tell me why You came to earth?

Jesus: To save the world.

Angel: How are You going to do this?

Jesus: I am going to die on a cross.

Angel: And then?

Jesus: I am going to rise from the dead and return to heaven.

Angel: But how will people know what You did for them?

Jesus: Well, I have 12 disciples whom I chose out of thousands. These men are going to be My agents of reconciliation and turn the world upside-down.

Angel: Watching them for the last three years hasn't impressed any of us angels. Are you going to give them Your master plan?

Jesus: What master plan?

Angel: Your detailed strategy for communicating the Gospel message with everyone on earth, changing the world and training others to do the same.

Jesus: I don't have a plan like that.

Angel: What are You going to do then?

Jesus: I will talk to them about relationship and what it means to abide in My love as I abide in My Father's love.

Honestly, I am so amazed to read what Jesus actually shared with His disciples just hours before He went to the cross to die. He discussed no master plan, schemes, fund-raising methods, building projects, spiritual laws or even Bible verses to memorize.

The entire chapter of John 15 is all about relationship—man's greatest problem since the Garden of Eden. It was there that our relationship with God was broken, and ever since, all our human relationships have been in total confusion as well. These were the two things Jesus talked about with His followers.

When we read this chapter in John, we could easily misunderstand that Jesus was instructing His disciples on bearing fruit, such as evangelism, witnessing, soul-winning and fulfilling the Great Commission. After all, He told them, "He who abides in Me, and I in him, bears much fruit" (John 15:5).

But what Jesus is actually referring to in this chapter is their lives. He is showing them how they will be able to produce the fruit of the Spirit mentioned in Galatians 5:22–23: "love, joy, peace, longsuffering, kindness, goodness, faithfulness, gentleness, self-control. Against such there is no law."

What Jesus is concentrating on here is not at all the kingdom work that you and I do nor the work the disciples were going to do later on in the book of Acts. The fruit we will bear if we abide in Him is transformed lives. All we do is simply the result of what we have become.

What Jesus explained to His disciples worked so well that we read later on in Acts 17:6, "These who have turned the world upside down have come here too."

A transformed life will impact everything around it and produce eternal results, without a single struggle to make it happen.

Henry Stanley, a worldly reporter, was sent to the jungles of Africa in search of David Livingstone. The last time the old missionary had been seen was seven years before when he returned to Africa in 1865. Finally, when Stanley found Livingstone in the middle of nowhere, the encounter changed him completely.

> ◡ *A* transformed life *will impact*
> *everything around it and produce*
> eternal results, *without a single struggle*
> *to make it happen.* ◡

Stanley lived with Livingstone for four months, sharing the same hut and every part of his life as well. He watched him closely and listened to his words. To his amazement, he could find no fault in this man. Up to that point, Stanley had been very critical of religion and even described himself as the worst infidel in London. But there in the jungle he encountered a man who simply lived out the words of Jesus: "Leave all and follow Me" (see Luke 18:22). Seeing Livingstone's love, his zeal and his commitment, Stanley's heart changed. "I was converted by him," he wrote, "although he had not tried to do it."

With all the frantic activities of modern-day Christianity, it is time for us to learn that it is not the plans we make or the programs that matter most, but the simple truth of letting His life flow through us.

Don't let it end. The journey continues . . .

If this book has been a blessing,
I would really like to hear from you.
Please send me an email at kp@gfa.org.

Notes

Chapter 8: Striving for Unity
1. Paul E. Billheimer, *Destined for the Throne*, rev. ed. (Minneapolis, MN: Bethany House Publishers, 1996), p. 22.

Chapter 9: Here Comes God with the Pruning Shears
1. Saint John of the Cross, *The Dark Night of the Soul* (New York: Doubleday, 1959).

Chapter 12: Peace through Humility
1. Roy Hession, *The Calvary Road* (Fort Washington, PA: CLC Publications, 1950).
2. Andrew Murray, *Humility: The Beauty of Holiness* (Old Tappan, NJ: Fleming H. Revell Company, n.d.), pp. 12, 13, 71.

Chapter 15: Which Road Will You Travel On?
1. Amy Carmichael, "Make Me Thy Fuel" taken from *Mountain Breezes* (Fort Washington, PA: CLC Publications, 1999), p. 223. Used with permission.

CHAPTER 20: What's the "One Thing"?
1. Amy Carmichael, *If* (London: SPCK Publishing, 1951), p. 37.

CHAPTER 25: The Weapon of Disunity
1. Paul E. Billheimer, *Love Covers* (Fort Washington, PA: Christian Literature Crusade, 1981), p. 7.

CHAPTER 28: Expand Your Borders
1. Hession, *The Calvary Road*.

CHAPTER 30: With Each Stroke of the Brush
1. "Let the Beauty of Jesus," Albert Orsborn © 1930 SP&S/Admin by Song Solutions CopyCare, 14 Horsted Square, Uckfield, East Sussex, TN21 8QG info@songsolutions.org. Used with permission.

CHAPTER 32: Destroying Deception
1. C.S. Lewis, *The Silver Chair* (New York: Macmillan Publishing Company, 1970), pp. 136–148.

CHAPTER 35: A Gospel of Great Joy
1. *The Visual Bible: Matthew*. Produced by Atila Bala and directed by Regardt van den Bergh, 240 min. Visual Bible. 1993. DVD.

GOSPEL FOR ASIA

After 2,000 years of Christianity, how can it be that nearly 3 billion people are still unreached with the Gospel? How long must they wait?

This is why Gospel for Asia exists.

More than 25 years ago, God specifically called us to invest our lives to reach the most unreached of South Asia through training and sending out national missionaries.

Gospel for Asia (GFA) is a missions organization dedicated to reaching the most unreached in the 10/40 Window. Thousands of GFA-supported pastors and missionaries serve full-time to share the love of Christ in 10 Asian countries.

National missionaries are highly effective because they work in their own or a similar culture. They already know, or can easily learn, the language, customs and culture of the people to whom they minister. They don't need visas, and they live economically at the same level as their neighbors. These advantages make them one of the fastest and most effective ways to get the Gospel to the millions who are still waiting to hear.

However, the young, economically weak Asian Church and her missionaries can't do it alone. The enormous task of reaching nearly 3 billion people takes the help of the whole Body of Christ worldwide.

That is why GFA offers those who cannot go themselves the opportunity to become senders and prayer partners of national missionaries—together fulfilling the Great Commission and sharing in the eternal harvest of souls.

To find out more information about Gospel for Asia or to receive a free copy of K.P. Yohannan's best-selling book *Revolution in World Missions*, visit our website at www.gfa.org or contact one of our offices near you.

AUSTRALIA P.O. Box 3587, Village Fair, Toowoomba QLD 4350
 Phone: 1300 889 339   Email: infoaust@gfa.org

CANADA 245 King Street E, Stoney Creek, ON L8G 1L9
 Toll free: 1-888-WIN-ASIA Email: infocanada@gfa.org

GERMANY Postfach 13 60, 79603 Rheinfelden (Baden)
 Phone: 07623 79 74 77   Email: infogermany@gfa.org

KOREA P.O. Box 984, Yeouido, Seoul 150-609
 Toll free: (080) 801-0191   Email: infokorea@gfa.org

NEW ZEALAND PO Box 302580, North Harbour, North Shore City 0751
 Toll free: 0508-918-918   Email: infonz@gfa.org

SOUTH AFRICA P.O. Box 28880, Sunridge Park, Port Elizabeth 6008
 Phone: 041 360-0198   Email: infoza@gfa.org

UNITED KINGDOM PO Box 166, Winterscale House, YORK YO10 5WA
 Freephone: 0800 032 8717   Email: infouk@gfa.org

UNITED STATES 1800 Golden Trail Court, Carrollton, TX 75010
 Toll free: 1-800-WIN-ASIA Email: info@gfa.org

SEND A NATIONAL MISSIONARY TODAY!

I want to help national missionaries reach their own people for Jesus.

I understand that it takes from US$120–US$210 a month to fully support a national missionary, including family support and ministry expenses.

TO BEGIN SPONSORING TODAY,

Visit our website at **WWW.GFA.ORG**

or call us at your nearest GFA office
Phone numbers are listed on page 170.

or fill out the form below and mail to the nearest GFA office.
National office addresses are listed on page 170.

❑ Starting now, I will prayerfully help support _____ national missionary(ies)
at $30[†] each per month = $_____ a month.

You'll receive a photo and testimony of each missionary you help sponsor.

❑ Please send me more information about how to help sponsor a national missionary.

Please circle: Mr. Mrs. Miss Rev.

Name _____

Address _____

City _____ State/Province/County _____

Zip/Postal Code _____ Country _____ Phone (_____) _____

Email _____

❑ Please send me free email updates.

HA9A-RB8S   ZHZA-RB8S

A higher standard.
A higher purpose.

Gospel for Asia sends 100 percent of your missionary support to the mission field. Nothing is taken out for administrative expenses.

† AUS $40, CAN $30, €30, CHF60, NZ $40, UK £20, ZA R150.

FREE EMAIL UPDATES
Sign up today at www.gfa.org

Hear from today's heroes of the mission field.
Have their stories and prayer requests sent straight to your inbox.

GOSPEL FOR ASIA UPDATE — SPONSOR A MISSIONARY

January 10, 2006 | Vol. V Issue 37 | Archives | My Account — 220,000 Subscribed

Dear Friend in Christ,

The desire of Gospel for Asia native missionaries is to reach as many lost souls as they can with the Gospel. Therefore, one of the most fulfilling times in their lives occurs when they are able to enter a village for the first time, carrying with them the Good News of Jesus Christ.

GFA mobile teams play a big part in helping missionaries spread the Gospel to more villages. Mobile teams spend about a week with local missionaries and pastors, going with them to nearby villages that have yet to be reached. They talk about Jesus with any who will listen and pass out Gospel tracts. In the evenings they show *Man of Mercy*, a film on the life of Jesus.

When the mobile team moves on to another village, they leave behind fertile ground. Some villagers will be very interested in the Gospel after seeing the film. Others will have already received salvation. Mobile teams prepare the way for local missionaries to plant more churches.

Click here to see a PhotoShow about the significant impact a mobile team's visit had on GFA Pastor Raji's ministry.

Yours for the unreached villages,

K.P. Yohannan

Founder & President
Gospel for Asia

- **Fuel your prayer life with compelling news and photos from the mission field.**
- **Stay informed with links to important video and audio clips.**
- **Learn about the latest opportunities to reach the lost world.**

GFA sends updates every week. You may cancel your free subscription at any time. We will not sell or release your email address for any reason.

MATERIALS FROM GOSPEL FOR ASIA

REVOLUTION IN WORLD MISSIONS

Step into the story of missionary statesman K.P. Yohannan and experience the world through his eyes. You will hang on every word—from the villages of India to the shores of Europe and North America. Watch out: His passion is contagious!

TOUCHING GODLINESS THROUGH SUBMISSION

It is not enough to watch others touch godliness—it is for *you*. With his engaging style, K.P. Yohannan challenges us that we, too, can follow Christ down this path of submission, in the end finding God's best.

THE ROAD TO REALITY

K.P. Yohannan gives an uncompromising call to live a life of simplicity to fulfill the Great Commission.

Order online at *www.gfa.org*

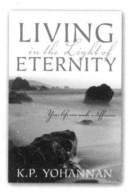

LIVING IN THE LIGHT OF ETERNITY

K.P. Yohannan lovingly, yet candidly, reminds Christians of their primary role while here on earth: harvesting souls. This book challenges us to look at our heart attitudes, motivation and our impact on eternity.

DESTINED TO SOAR

Does it feel like life is closing in on you? K.P. Yohannan shows you the way to rise above the weight of this world and keep your true purpose in clear view. Relevant and incredibly practical, his hope-filled approach to critical issues frees you to be all for Jesus.

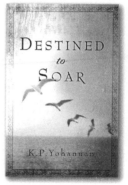

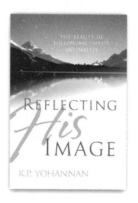

REFLECTING HIS IMAGE

K.P. Yohannan takes us on a journey back to God's original purpose for each of our lives: to reflect His image. This book is a compilation of short, easy-to-read chapters that all deal with following Christ closely.

Order online at *www.gfa.org*

AGAINST THE WIND

In this eye-opening book, K.P. Yohannan challenges you to consider how you are running the race God has set before you. Like the apostle Paul, you too can learn what it takes to be able to one day say, "I have fought the good fight; I have finished the race; I have kept the faith" no matter what the obstacles.

COME, LET'S REACH THE WORLD

How effective are the Church's current missions strategies? Are the unreached hearing the Gospel? K.P. Yohannan examines the traditional approach to missions—its underlying assumptions, history and fruit—in light of Scripture and the changing world scene. This book is a strong plea for the Body of Christ to partner with indigenous missionaries so that the whole world may hear.

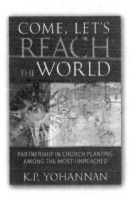

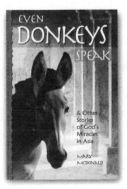

EVEN DONKEYS SPEAK

This children's book is a collection of stories taken straight from the mission fields of South Asia. As you read these exciting tales of God at work, you and your youngsters will feel as if you are right there with these believers, following the Lord amid the steaming jungles and cold mountain villages of Asia. It's great reading, no matter your age.

EXCITING DVDs

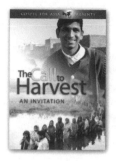

THE CALL TO HARVEST

In this 25-minute DVD, you'll meet the people who are near to the Father's heart: the unreached. See them through the eyes of national missionaries like Titus and Joseph, who face danger and hardship to preach the Gospel in Asia. As the life-giving presence of Jesus transforms lives and families daily, the Lord is calling His people everywhere to come and share the joy of this harvest.

TOUCH OF LOVE

You will be inspired as K.P. Yohannan takes you around the world to see the "Untouchable" children of Asia through Jesus' eyes. His message will help you better understand the heart of Christ, who calls these children His own—and give you a chance to reach them with His eternal love.

TO LIVE IS CHRIST!

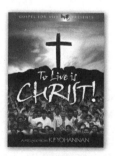

Feel the passion of K.P. Yohannan as he describes the life-giving power of total commitment to Christ in this 55-minute DVD. Be amazed by stories of missionaries who risk their lives to preach the Gospel. Weep with him as he recalls his mother's years of sacrifice that changed lives for eternity. Many people search in vain for the path that leads to the abundant life that Jesus promised. K.P., through the Word of God, uncovers that path in this inspiring and challenging message.

Order online at *www.gfa.org*